MYSTICISM AND
THE MODERN MIND

I CANNOT accept any definition which identifies mysticism with excited or hysterical emotionalism, with sublimated eroticism, with visions and revelations, with supernatural (dualistically opposed to natural) activities, nor, on the philosophical side, with irrationalism.

WILLIAM RALPH INGE [1]

TRUST thyself: every heart vibrates to that iron string. Accept the place the divine providence has found for you, the society of your contemporaries, the connection of events. Great men have always done so, and confided themselves childlike to the genius of their age, betraying their perception that the absolutely trustworthy was seated at their heart, working through their hands, predominating in all their being. And we are now men, and must accept in the highest mind the same transcendent destiny; and not minors and invalids in a protected corner, not cowards fleeing before a revolution, but guides, redeemers and benefactors, obeying the Almighty effort and advancing on Chaos and the Dark.

RALPH WALDO EMERSON [2]

[1] W. R. Inge, *Mysticism in Religion* (Chicago, 1948), p. 154.
[2] Brooks Atkinson (ed.), *The Complete Essays and Writings of Ralph Waldo Emerson* (New York, 1940), pp. 146-7.

MYSTICISM AND
THE MODERN MIND

Edited by
ALFRED P. STIERNOTTE
Assistant Professor of Philosophy, Quinnipiac College

THE LIBERAL ARTS PRESS
NEW YORK

Published at 153 West 72nd Street, New York 23, N. Y.

Printed in the United States of America

FOREWORD

This symposium has the purpose of presenting an exploration of, rather than an anthology on, mysticism, since a number of excellent compilations already exist. A careful selection of material to appeal to the modern mind has been attempted, especially that modern mind dissatisfied with excessive claims by mystics in the familiar religious traditions. The symposium may therefore be significant for what it omits as well as for what it includes.

I wish to express my sincere appreciation to the contributors who rallied enthusiastically to this project. I wish especially to thank Professor John A. Irving, Chairman, Department of Philosophy, Victoria College, University of Toronto, who made important suggestions for the inclusion of certain chapters in this symposium. I am particularly indebted for the chapter on ontological and ethical mysticism in Indian thought by Dr. N. A. Nikam, Professor of Philosophy, University of Mysore; Secretary, Indian Philosophical Congress; and Visiting Fellow, Yale University, 1952-53. Without this important study by an authority on Eastern mysticism and philosophy this symposium would have been decidedly deficient. I also appreciate the interesting approach to the relation of logical analysis and mysticism by Professor Irving who infused into it his great knowledge of a school of philosophy which has often been vigorously critical of mystical and metaphysical presuppositions. It would appear, however, as he has happily indicated, that some aspects of Wittgenstein's logic are not at all inimical to the mystical quest.

The philosophy of Existentialism, which may be of increasing relevance and importance in this country, has its relation to mysticism as presented by Professors Newton P. Stallknecht and Henry Nelson Wieman. I am happy that some aspects of this many-sided philosophy, Existentialism, have been elaborated by pens far more competent than mine.

To all contributors may I express once more my deep gratitude for their generous co-operation in a work designed to convey an interpretation of the mystical consciousness in terms of philosophical trends usually neglected in such discussions.

ALFRED P. STIERNOTTE

New Haven, Connecticut
April 1959

CONTENTS

ACKNOWLEDGMENTS

I am grateful to the following publishers and editors for permission to quote from works for which they hold the copyright:

Harcourt, Brace and Company, Inc., New York, for permission to quote several lines from "Burnt Norton" in *Collected Poems 1909-1935* by T. S. Eliot, copyright 1936, in the chapter by Professor Newton P. Stallknecht.

Librairie Payot, Paris, and Professor Jean Wahl, Université de Paris, for quotations from Jean Wahl, *Traité de Metaphysique*.

Professor Paul Weiss, Editor, *The Review of Metaphysics*, Yale University, New Haven, Conn., for Professor Stallknecht's incorporation of several passages from his reviews of Wahl, Chaix-Ruy, and Marcel published in *The Review of Metaphysics*, June 1954, September 1954, and June 1955.

New Directions, Norfolk, Conn., for permission to quote from *Nausea* by Jean-Paul Sartre.

Mr. T. N. Venkataraman, Manager-President, Śri Ramanasramam, Tiruvannamalai, India, for quotations from *Maharshi's Gospel,* Books I and II, and *Talks with Śri Ramana Maharshi,* Vol. I.

Navajivan Trust, Ahmedabad, India, for quotations from M. K. Gandhi, *Hindu Dharma.*

Śri Aurobindo Ashram, Pondicherry, India, for quotations from *Synthesis of Yoga* by Śri Aurobindo.

George Allen & Unwin Limited, London, England, for quotations from S. Radhakrishnan, editor, *The Principal Upaniṣads,* and from *Dattatreya: The Way and the Goal* by His Highness Śri Jaya Chamarajendra Wadiyar Bahadur.

Oxford University Press, Bombay, India, for quotations from

The Thirteen Principal Upanishads translated by Robert Ernest Hume.

Brandt & Brandt, New York, for permission to quote a few lines from *Renascence and Other Poems,* published by Harper & Brothers, and copyright 1912, 1940 by Edna St. Vincent Millay.

Yale University Press, New Haven, Connecticut, for quotations from Karl Jaspers, *Way to Wisdom.*

Rider and Company, London, England, for quotations from *Selected Writings of D. T. Suzuki,* edited by William Barrett and published by Doubleday and Company, New York.

Routledge and Kegan Paul Limited, London, England, for quotations from Ludwig Wittgenstein, *Tractatus Logico-Philosophicus.*

Dr. John Haynes Holmes, Minister Emeritus, The Community Church, New York, for permission to use a passage from *The Beacon Song and Service Book,* published by The Beacon Press, Boston.

The Macmillan Company, New York, for quotations from Henry Nelson Wieman, *Religious Experience and Scientific Method* and from A. N. Whitehead, *Religion in the Making.*

E. P. Dutton & Company, Inc., New York, for quotations from *The Life Divine* by Śri Aurobindo, copyright 1949, 1951 by Śri Aurobindo Library, Inc.

The Meeting House Press, Boston, for permission to use a revised version of some material in *Man's Hidden Search* in Rev. Kenneth L. Patton's chapter, "Mysticism and Naturalistic Humanism."

MYSTICISM AND
THE MODERN MIND

MYSTICISM AND THE MODERN MIND

ALFRED P. STIERNOTTE

A WORK DEVOTED to a modern approach to mysticism may seem incongruous and possibly escapist to many liberals influenced by a scientific study of religion as well as by the exploration of programs designed to lessen injustice and promote greater social harmony. Surely, it will be said, what we need at this time is not a presentation of something as dubious, vague, or retrograde as mysticism! Surely what we need is a new formulation of religious philosophy which will shed some light on such contentious problems as the conflicting aspects of neo-naturalism and neo-orthodoxy. In the face of the present confusion as to the many rival claims of different types of religious thought, it would be better to devote more attention to the elucidation of these bewildering factors in our religious philosophy so that with fresh vigor we would be able to achieve a sensible and convincing orientation.

The more practical-minded among our liberals may claim that mysticism is the mark of the indolent, the indifferent, of those who, harassed or frightened by the complexity of the present scene, wish to escape to a spiritual oasis of their own and enjoy surreptitiously the fruits of its verdure in the midst of a desert of social tensions and human desolation from which they avert their gaze! These liberals may claim that the attempt to interpret life in mystical terms, in the sense of inexplicable and incomprehensible mysterious forces somehow or other rendered acceptable through traditional or esoteric symbolism, is in fact a negation of the desirable effort to understand life rationally and thereby to be able to lessen, and perhaps control, its conflicts. Surely, it will be said, the presumption of the achievement of an inner ecstatic experience, divorced from concern with the trials and tribulations

3

of men, separated from the urgent task of maintaining democratic values against the dangers of totalitarianism, is nothing less than the enjoyment of a pernicious type of spiritual egotism—nothing less than the betrayal of humanity! Some of our ardent social reformers will have nothing to do with what they call an otherworldly mysticism, regarding it much more as the negation of Schweitzer's dictum of "reverence for life" than its affirmation. Rather than be engulfed in introspective, self-regarding experience, with its false implication of spiritual superiority, let us be absorbed, they will say, in the present struggle so that, inspired with the riches of our ancient Hebrew tradition, we may condemn "wickedness in high places," and resolve "to loose the bonds of wickedness, to undo the heavy burdens, and to let the oppressed go free!"

Again, important psychological studies of the mystical experience have brought to light the fact that what was imagined to be so innocent was in some instances the fantasy of a deranged, frustrated, or pathological personality. It is also well known that there are aspects of Eastern mysticism in which the concentration of one's consciousness upon a formless void is held to be the very culmination of the experience.[1] Also, the mystics of the Christian tradition have made claims of direct contact with heavenly beings and even of union with the Deity which the modern spirit, so often accused of arrogance, would approach in a much humbler mood.

Let it be emphasized at the outset that the mysticism with which we are concerned is not completely defined by descriptions of the experience in terms of contact with a circumambient realm of spiritual essences dwelling in some supernatural domain. Nor has it anything to do with the absurd presumptions of occultists with respect to powers of divine revelation possessed by some mystical "superphysical elite." Nor is it concerned with the denial of the scientific method as properly understood. Nor is its special

[1] For a discussion of the meaning of void or emptiness in Eastern mysticism see D. T. Suzuki, *Mysticism: Christian and Buddhist* (New York, 1957), pp. 26-30. Note: "Emptiness is not a vacancy, it holds in it infinite rays of light and swallows all the multiplicities there are in this world." (P. 30.)

attraction the achievement of some inner joy, "peace of mind," wherein the soul is liberated from the tensions and exasperations of our time.

What, then, are the criteria of a modern approach to mysticism which may hope to avoid the excessive claims of the mystical tradition in its quest for some measure of invulnerability from its opponents? It would be rash for anyone to state precisely what these criteria are. The subject deserves exploration, and it is to be hoped that the present volume will shed a modicum of light on what the mystical mood may mean for men of our tempestuous period.

It may be urged that the crucial aspect of the mystical consciousness is its intense realization of meaningful patterns in the universe, life, and history so that the meanings so apprehended glow with a sublime fire in the inner soul and give to the person so favored an ineffable sense of the wonder, beauty, glory, and unity of the Ultimate—that Being which is alike the concern of philosopher and mystic. Indeed, the mystics testify to the resolution of all meanings and patterns in an experience of ecstatic union with ultimate reality. The particular theological and philosophical framework in which this experience has been expressed we shall consider a secondary matter. Surely those who have had glimpses of the mystical consciousness and are yet aware of the critical temper of our times will be reluctant to agree that their experience is spurious unless couched in the terminology of the great mystics of the Christian, Jewish, Moslem, Hindu, or any other religious tradition. We pay our profound respects to the great mystics of the ages, whose contributions have been adequately described by Evelyn Underhill, Charles A. Bennett, Rufus M. Jones, Thomas Hywell Hughes, Sir Francis Younghusband, Rudolf Otto, W. T. Stace, William Ralph Inge, E. Récéjac, H. Delacroix, James H. Leuba, William James, James B. Pratt, and Gershom G. Scholem—to mention just a few of the more eminent investigators. But is it not time to explore what the experience might mean to a religious liberal of our own day, fully aware of the frailties and failures of traditional religion and traditional mysticism, and whose approach to the spiritual life is grounded in

some form of naturalism? Even such an outstanding exponent of
Christian mysticism as Evelyn Underhill is willing to admit "that
mysticism enjoys the patronage of many pious monists and philosophic naturalists." [2] And it must be remembered that naturalism
is not necessarily agnostic or antitheistic; there is a theistic
naturalism expressed in the works of H. N. Wieman and other
empirical theologians. The extremely sympathetic discussion of
mysticism by the pragmatic philosopher Irwin Edman in *Four
Ways of Philosophy* is another indication that the mystical experience is one which can be interpreted in terms of new philosophical horizons.

In thus orienting this symposium to philosophy rather than to
the study of the psychological mystical experience and the religious tradition in which it is found, we are encouraged by the
remarks of Charles A. Bennett: "Philosophy is the articulation
and completion of mysticism, but mysticism, in turn, is needed
in order to complete by correction and supplementation the work
of philosophy." [3]

If there is one conviction which underlies the many varieties of

[2] Evelyn Underhill, *Mysticism,* 12th ed. (London, 1930), p. 43. It is no dis-
paragement of the greatness of this work as an exposition of Christian mysticism to indicate its dogmatic character in certain instances: "No one needs,
I suppose, to be told that the two chief features of Christian schematic theology are the dogmas of the Trinity and the Incarnation. They correlate and
explain each other: forming together, for the Christian, the 'final key' to the
riddle of the world. The history of practical and institutional Christianity is
the history of the attempt to exhibit their meaning in space and time. The
history of mystical philosophy is the history—still incomplete—of the demon-
stration of their meaning in eternity." *Ibid.,* p. 107. Obviously the present
symposium is an attempt to transcend these limitations of dogmatic theology,
and is much more in agreement with the following affirmation from John
Laird: "Nature-pantheists, who are only and strictly Nature-pantheists, are
surely entitled to say that they do experience awe, reverence, wonder and
mystery for Nature herself, that they also are among the mystics and are not
mere wand-bearers; and the like. It is simply not true that a mystic must be
either a supra-mondane theist or a hypertheist; and it is not at all clear that
he must be a theist of any intelligible sort." "Theism and Hypertheism,"
Harvard Theological Review, XXXVI, No. 1 (January, 1943), 79.

[3] Charles A. Bennett, *A Philosophical Study of Mysticism* (New Haven,
1923), p. 7.

the modern liberal religious temper, it is that the universe is not some static, soulless mechanism but rather a dynamic, creative process from which relations, meanings, values, ideals, and spiritual personalities emerge. In the words of Emerson, we discover anew that "the world lies no longer a dull miscellany and lumber-room, but has form and order; there is no trifle, there is no puzzle, but one design unites and animates the farthest pinnacle and the lowest trench."

The orientation of the liberal mind to the riches latent in our own mystical tradition—in which Emerson surely has a distinct place—is yet to be made. For we forget too easily that justly celebrated address on *The American Scholar* in which Emerson held forth as the potential possession of all men a sublime truth which is close to the mystical vision:

> The scholar is that man who must take up into himself all the ability of the time, all the contributions of the past, all the hopes of the future. He must be an university of knowledges. If there be one lesson more than another which should pierce his ear, it is, The world is nothing, the man is all; in yourself is the law of all nature . . . in yourself slumbers the whole of Reason; it is for you to know all; it is for you to dare all.

This exalted possibility of knowing all and doing all—an Emersonian hyperbole, to be sure—of discovering the culmination of the law of nature in man, of rejoicing in the pattern of Being in which man shares, is a fascinating vision for the present symposium. This series of essays attempts to clarify and to formulate just what we mean by mysticism and the modern mind, what aspects of mysticism, what philosophical and religious doctrines may still be valid when the acids of modernity have done their worst. In no sense do the contributors claim any finality for their various expressions. Finalities and absolutes are losing their appeal in our transient world—without at the same time leaving us at the mercy of a universe of chance, unpredictability, or of pessimism. No theological or philosophical uniformity has been required of the contributors beyond the expression of what constitutes for them a defensible presentation of mysticism in our time.

It is felt by many of the contributors that mysticism cannot be held within the confines of the Christian religion, though several have pointed to significant insights derived from this tradition. Others were forceful in rejecting theological formulae and stressed ethical and humanistic values as significant for an adequate and credible exposition of the kind of mysticism they favor.[4] That a profound ethical implication is not necessarily divorced from ontological reference is cogently argued by Professor N. A. Nikam, Department of Philosophy, Mysore University, India, whose great knowledge of his own glorious Hindu tradition, expressed in many relevant quotations from the Upanishads, is an indisputable affirmation of the mysticism of the East.

There is one group, however, among those who call themselves modern, especially in a philosophical sense, who might regard the present attempt to relate mysticism to Christian, non-Christian, naturalistic, and evolutionary philosophies, as destined to end, as all metaphysical inquiries, they would urge, inevitably end, in— meaninglessness! This group is represented by the Vienna circle of logical positivists and their disciples, and whether positivism implies a total negation of any type of metaphysical inquiry would involve a discussion beyond the confines of this symposium. It would appear, however, that positivism does not imply a denial of mysticism, for one of the leading philosophers of this school, Ludwig Wittgenstein, did pay his respects to the mystical consciousness in one of his important logical studies. The way in which Wittgenstein did this is explained persuasively by Professor John A. Irving, long a student of the logical philosophy of Wittgenstein.

This symposium is not, therefore, oriented to any one religious or philosophical tradition. The reader who believes that mysticism is pre-eminently the province of the Christian religion will be surprised, perhaps exasperated, perhaps enlightened, to find

[4] That mysticism may be used as a protest against restrictive theological doctrines is an important point raised by Paul Tillich: "Mysticism has criticized the demonically distorted sacramental-priestly substance by devaluating every medium of revelation and by trying to unite the soul directly with the ground of being, to make it enter the mystery of existence without the help of a finite medium." *Systematic Theology* (Chicago, 1951), p. 140.

convincing presentations of mysticism in non-Christian religions, and some suggested by modern evolutionary philosophies whose full religious import is at present being developed but needs further supplementation. The reader who imagines that absolute idealism is the one philosophical melting pot for all varieties of mysticism will find other systems in this work, especially systems of creative and emergent evolution, to be evaluated on their own merit. Furthermore, the reader who expects to discover in this volume a fantastic array of esoteric disciplines or secret doctrines will be sadly disappointed, for it cannot be too strongly emphasized that the editor and all contributors are firmly of the opinion that mysticism can be given new life only by a ruthless rejection of any esoteric and occult encumbrances accumulated from the past. Only thus will mysticism gain any hearing from the modern mind.

Finally, the reader need not imagine that he must be conversant to an excessive degree with technical issues in philosophy and the abstract battles of the schools which delight philosophers, in order to comprehend this symposium. In the words of Paul Weiss, he need not forego "the pleasure of trying out some posture in the perpetual ballet of the schools," [5] as the ballet will not be too involved! Rather, may he find encouragement from W. T. Stace's remark: "Our supposition is that mystic intuition exists in all men, but that in the great mystic it is developed in an abnormal degree." [6]

Mysticism is essentially democratic—not esoteric!

[5] Paul Weiss, *Man's Freedom* (New Haven, 1950), p. 7.
[6] W. T. Stace, *Time and Eternity* (Princeton, 1952), p. 67.

MYSTICISM

JOHN HAYNES HOLMES

All I know, all I want to know is that I have found in my relations with my fellow men and in my glad beholding of the universe
a reality of truth, goodness and beauty, and that I am trying to
make my life as best I can a dedication to this reality. When I am
in the thinking mood, I try to be rigorously rational, and thus not
to go one step farther in my thoughts and language than my reason
can take me. I then become uncertain as to whether I or any man
can assert much about God, and fall back content into the mood of
Job. When, however, in preaching or in prayer, in some high moment of inner communion or of profound experience with life
among my fellows, I feel the pulse of emotion suddenly beating in
my heart, and I am lifted up as though upon some sweeping tide
that is more than the sluggish current of my days, I find it easy to
speak as the poets speak, and cry, as so many of them cry, to God.
But when I say "God," it is poetry and not theology. Nothing
that any theologian ever wrote about God has helped me much, but
everything that the poets have written about flowers, and birds, and
skies, and seas, and the saviors of the race, and God—whoever he
may be—has at one time or another reached my soul! More and
more, as I grow older, I live in the lovely thought of these seers and
prophets. The theologians gather dust upon the shelves of my
library, but the poets are stained with my fingers and blotted with
my tears. I never seem so near truth as when I care not what I think
or believe, but only with these masters of inner vision would live
forever.[1]

MYSTICISM MEANS to me the belief in and practice of direct
communion with God. The deep-rooted tradition of
Christianity affirms the necessity of mediation between
the soul and God. The Gnostics, finding a direct approach of the
human to the divine as incredible as the natural scientist today

[1] J. H. Holmes, "A Modern Faith," *The Beacon Song and Service Book*
(Boston, 1935), p. 72.

finds the relationship between mind and brain, built up a kind of ladder of intermediary contact between man and the deity he worshiped. The broad stream of Christian orthodoxy has presented the church, or the Bible, or Jesus the Christ as the means by which God could be found and understood. Only the heretics of mysticism have dared to affirm that the way to God is open. Turn inward, and there find the indwelling Spirit! Or upward, and there discover the Over-Soul! In either case God is at hand, to be found of those who seek him. "Ask, and it shall be given you; seek, and ye shall find; knock, and it shall be opened unto you."

I

If mysticism has not established itself as a part of the accepted body of Christian experience, it is because it defies the accepted standards of verification, or indeed any verification at all. It may well be argued that mysticism, by its very nature, constitutes its own verification. But such a contention does not carry us very far in an age dominated by the principles and methods of contemporary science. When a laboratory worker in any part of the world announces the discovery of some new truth, we may be sure that he has not made his statement until he has exhausted every means of verification at his disposal. Even so, the new announcement is not accepted until other scientists in other parts of the world repeat their colleague's experiments, and test the results by new experiments of their own. Only when this repetitive work has produced invariably the same phenomena—in other words, has verified the new truth—is this truth definitely accepted as one more extension of the great body of human knowledge.

Now, mysticism is not susceptible to verification of this kind. Each mystical experience is unique to a single individual, acting in one very particular set of conditions. This set of conditions cannot be repeated, nor the individual in question duplicated. What he has seen, or heard, or felt, has an intensity and therefore a reality which well-nigh defies description. But to another individual this experience remains a mere report, at second or even third hand, which is quite as likely to be a record of personal

illusion as of general knowledge. Surely, we cannot take the
stories of countless individuals, unverified and unverifiable, and
adopt them on their own say-so into the vital substance of truth.
In certain cases, the character of a particular witness, the quality
of his testimony, the inherent nature of his experience, may com-
bine to accredit a certain feeling of integrity which tempts us to
give sanction to the material offered for our consideration. But
nothing is quite so fatal to the quest of truth as personal prefer-
ences or concessions. If we are not to go hopelessly astray, we
must keep ourselves rigorously bound to objective standards. The
road to truth, whatever else it may or may not be, is strictly impersonal. And mysticism remains the most intensely personal
thing in all the world.

II

Yet there is a verification, or at least a confirmation, of mystical
experience which is not to be neglected or ignored. I refer to what
I may call an identity of witness which makes mysticism to be
something far more and better than the vagrant word of irresponsible individuals.

Mystics have appeared in all ages and among all peoples. They
have endured ecstasies of rapture—seen visions and dreamed
dreams which have lifted their souls to far-flung spaces of the
soul. Most of these mystics have been as lonely as Zarathustra in
his cave. Some of them have been as companionable as St. Francis,
strewing the ways of common life with "little flowers" of the
spirit. Many of them, like Swedenborg, have been great scholars
and preachers, and have imparted their testimonies to chosen
bands of students or to vast multitudes of hearers. But all of them
have been—originals. Their words have sprung from their own
inmost beings, and therewith have had a distinction of character
which is unique. Yet have they revealed the same truths, and
dealt with the same order of experience. In many cases it would
be possible to take the testimonies of one of these mystics and
substitute them for those of another, and have the substitution
remain undetected. This is the reason why a collection of mystical
utterances, an anthology of the type of Aldous Huxley's *A*

Perennial Philosophy, for example, presents so monotonous a course of reading. Having read one passage, we instinctively feel that we have read all.

This identity of thought and expression in men so different is particularly notable in the case of the more primitive mystics. These seers, or prophets—Lao-tse, for instance—have much of the color and tang of the societies which produced them. Each is as unique as palm and pine. But at bottom, in all that makes them mystics, and not merely philosophers and teachers, they are strangely alike. This fact we are tempted to explain by surmising that these men had contact with one another and shared ideas— or that travelers moved from country to country, and carried with them ideas, as they carried goods and merchandise, for purposes of exchange. In Plato we try to recognize material borrowed from the East. Because certain of Jesus' teachings seem not so different from those of Buddha, we imagine that, in his hidden years, the Nazarene may have journeyed to India and sat at the feet of her wise men as earlier he sat at the feet of Jewish doctors in the Temple. But we tend to exaggerate the degree of contact enjoyed and maintained by ancient civilizations. As a matter of fact, channels of communication in those early days were few. Travelers of the type of Herodotus or even Marco Polo were rare. Scrolls and parchments were seldom published and still more seldom conveyed abroad. If ancient mystics, like modern mystics, speak the same language, have the same experience, uncover the same depths of spiritual wisdom, it is not because they were in touch with one another and compared what they saw and heard as modern research workers compare experimental data. Characteristically, as we have stated, they were men who dwelt apart and sank deep within themselves, and were content with the witness of their own souls. Their identity springs from the fact that they drank from the same wellsprings of the spirit, unveiled the same light of truth, sought and found, within them and above, the same consciousness of God. They laid hold on the same oneness of reality, and were themselves made one.

It is thus that the mystics verify each other! More valid than any reproduction of phenomena within the laboratory is this coincidence of experience within the soul. Remote, solitary, silent, these mystics look on different skies and hold converse in different tongues. They know different cultures, and handle different elements of knowledge. What they see is denied to other men. It seems strange, fantastic. But the ages pass, the record holds, and lo, the single voice becomes a chorus of voices in strong and sweet accord. These mystics, for all their loneliness, were having a common experience and reporting a single truth. There is no variation, least of all any contradiction, in what at first hand they see and know. The witness of one confirms the witness of all the others. This is verification of the highest order. Than this great body of truth, I know of none more sure.

III

So the mystics are to be believed. Not literally in all cases. One must take with great seriousness the declaration of Theodore Parker that the elements of religious faith are so many intuitions of the soul. When Socrates refers to the demon within his breast as the guide of all his conduct, he is anticipating the utterly sober experience of Gandhi in hearing the inward voice of God as the Truth which he must follow. St. Francis had a sturdy common sense which like a compass needle pointed the way to the ineffable grace and beauty of his thinking. But the visions of Plotinus, like those of Blake, were a poetic interpretation of what the soul beheld, and the dreams of Swedenborg were largely a projection into the next world of the paraphernalia of this. Of the reality of one quite as much as of another, however, there can be no doubt. The mystics bring in various guises a testimony of God, the soul, and immortality which is unimpeachable. They give an authority to conscience and the moral law which is absolute. After the theologians have argued their way through to reasoned propositions of the mind which, however impressive, are never conclusive, there come these mystics with their direct encounter with Truth. Like "the pure in heart [who] see God," their word is final.

It is this which makes the mystics so much more important than the theologians or schoolmen. The latter argue and debate.

They lay down lines of thought and follow them through to
logical conclusions. They formulate intellectual propositions, and
analyze them into various implications of reality. They rear vast
theological systems, in the structures of which all their articles of
faith find place. These scholastic thinkers are akin to the philosophers. Indeed, in their best estate they are philosophers—that
particular group of philosophers who deal with the material of
religion rather than that of science, or politics, or ethical theory.
The distinctive aspect of their work, as of that of all philosophers,
is its rationalistic character. They depend upon reason as the chief
instrument in the inquiry after truth. Whatever reason can do,
they do; wherever it leads, they follow on. The achievements of
reason, in the theological as in other fields, must be ranked among
the supreme achievements of man. Reason is itself indispensable
to his thought and life. But reason is always second hand. It is
mechanical rather than vital, formal rather than real. It leaves as
artificially demonstrated what is not yet seen or known.

It is here that the mystics appear and offer their testimony,
which is that of experience rather than of thought. They report
what has become a part of their very lives. They describe, with
frequently faltering but always rapturous tongue, what they have
beheld as they behold the sun, breathed as they breathe the atmosphere, felt as they feel the beating of the blood stream in their
hearts. These mystics do not have to argue about God, for example. Why should they, when they have stood in his presence
and looked upon his face? They have no need to speculate about
the possibility or probability of the future life, when in this
present life they have entered into the mysteries of the eternal
spirit. As for conscience, it has the intimacy and authority of a
voice heard within the breast. How dare one question or disobey
it? It is the firsthand quality of experience, as contrasted with
speculation or more rational conviction, which gives the mystics
their peculiar power. They are like the poets who have no need
of argumentation now that they have broken through the barriers
of sense and entered into the full wonder of reality itself. Passed,
like Plato, from the realm of ideas into that of Ideals! These poets
have gotten through with discussion and debate. No longer bound

to earth with its trammels of pure and practical reason, they have taken wings and soared aloft into the vast empyrean of immediate apprehension. Their material is now the substance of dreams and visions. It is the invisible suddenly seen with an ineffable intensity of beauty. It is the temporal transfigured into the eternal, and become truth manifest. What they tell us is not a thesis but a report, radiant with rapturous emotion, of what they have been given to see "in Xanadu," where they

> . . . on honey-dew [have] fed,
> And drunk the milk of Paradise.

As with the poets, so with the mystics! Their experiences are identical. In the one case as in the other, these men, poets and mystics alike, speak with authority. For they have looked, at first "with holy dread" and then with "deep delight" upon the ultimate, and told us that it is so.

The mystics, therefore, are our primary source of religious truth. Yet in following the golden thread of religious history, we are trained to turn first to the theologians, and ignore the mystics. Thus, when the two characters are combined in the same person, as is not infrequently the case, we exalt the theologian at the expense of the mystic. St. Paul, for example, is given rank as the first and greatest of theologians, as though the mystical glory of his epistles were not his chief claim to fame. St. Augustine is remembered and consulted as one of the most profound of theologians, and largely forgotten as a mystic of extraordinary insight and outlook. We all recognize the magnificent rationalistic powers of Theodore Parker, but how many of us recall that the foundations of his faith were laid firm and sure in the divine intuitions of his soul. As for the course of history, it follows the line of the theologians and the ecclesiastics, with little more than side glances at the mystics. Yet in these latter flows the pure stream of inspiration. In the long period of the Dark Ages and the Middle Ages, the schoolmen kept alive the traditions of philosophy which carried back to Plato and Aristotle. The popes held together a society and civilization which all but fell to pieces in the decline and fall of the Roman Empire. In both instances, this was creative work of a high order, but fundamentally secular in character. The sacred influences of the church were perpetuated and kept at work by the monks and the mystics. In them run the true currents of Christian history. In a Bernard, a Francis, a Thomas a Kempis, a Boehme, a George Whitefield, and the American Transcendentalists lie the wellsprings from which these currents pour. Here lives religion—not in the doctrines of the sages, but in the visions of the seers.

IV

In mysticism, therefore, do we find the highest and truest expression of spiritual faith. It is a river of living water flowing to the vast ocean of eternal being, and fructifying all the country through which it moves. Yet just because it is a river unchecked and unguided in its course, it needs to be guarded from pollution, or from breaking into some wild flood which inundates and therewith destroys the landscape. Mysticism, in other words, has its deadly perils:

(1) Thus, it is constantly in danger of misunderstanding reason, and displacing it from its necessary controls of life. The essence of mysticism, of course, is feeling—the direct reaction of inner emotion upon outer experience. It is experience itself unfolding into the disclosure of its deeper meanings. Reason, per contra, is a process of thought, deliberately removed from direct contact with reality. It is the mind coolly and calmly at work upon phenomena in the quest of truth. In this purely objective inquiry, it seeks to avoid emotion as a corruptive force, and to this end subdues its activities to certain rationalistic principles which bring order out of chaos, and understanding out of ignorance and confusion. At first sight, it seems as though rationalism and mysticism were inherently opposed to one another. The one appears to be a form of bondage, the other pure freedom. The former is so indirect, even remote, in its approach to life, the latter so direct and thus immediate in its identification with life! Reason bears fetters which bind it to earth, while the soul takes wings and soars aloft.

But all this is superficial and far astray. For, as a matter of fact, these two attributes of man's being are not contradictory, but complementary. Certainly mysticism is as unsafe as an un-bridled horse if it abandons reason. More than any other activity of life, it needs and should cry out for the control and guidance of the mind. The bane of mysticism is fanaticism, even madness. Leave it to itself, and it twirls and twists, and gyrates, and in the end crashes, like an aeroplane, driven by potent engines, which leaps aloft with no pilot at the helm. No wonder that mysticism has again and again forfeited the confidence of sensible men. Its extravagances are beyond all reason. Which means that we need reason to correct the mystic experiences of the soul and hold them fast to the course of intelligent and therefore intelligible disclosures of truth! Reason and rapture need one another, the latter to drive and lift, the former to control and guide. Mysticism, in other words, must be rational, and therefore dwell with reason as the handmaiden of the spirit.

(2) A second danger is what Whitehead calls solitariness. The mystic seeks to be alone—naturally so, since it is not in society but in solitude that he can commune with the secrets of his own being. So, like Byron's Manfred, he flees to the mountains, where amid the snowy peaks he may meet the deeper spirit of his life. Or he loses himself in the desert, where in sandy wastes he may be undisturbed even of the wild creatures of the wilderness. The sea is a familiar haunt of the dreamer, for the very vastness of its waters carries the soul to far spaces beyond itself. Night with its myriad stars brings the silence in which inner voices may speak. So does the mystic avoid the crowd. Gandhi, doomed to mingle with the multitudes, saved his life and kept his vision clear by practicing in each week a day of silence.

But there is danger in this practice of retirement. For one thing, it may so easily become a form of self-indulgence. To keep touch with men is inevitably to give oneself to the service of their needs and the comforting of their distress, whereas in solitude one can minister only to one's own life. So that one becomes self-centered and in the end completely selfish. It is in this sense that aloneness becomes an escape from the demands and the duties of existence. The mystic flees to mountain and desert in the be-ginning to commune with God and therewith restore his soul.

Then, like the creeping inroads of a disease, idleness becomes pleasant, silence soothing, and the world's exactions happily remote. Thus, step by step, a good life becomes a sterile life, and bitterness as of brackish water the poison of the soul. What is necessary, of course, is a balance in these relations. There must be a dual contact with God and man, a moving easily and regularly from the one to the other, making them to be in the end a unity of experience. Jesus accomplished this ideal in his retirement to the mountains or the distant lake shore for relief after exhausting hours with the people. "It is easy," writes Emerson in his essay on *Self-Reliance,* "in the world to live after the world's opinion; it is easy in solitude to live after our own; but the great man is he who in the midst of the crowd keeps with perfect sweetness the independence of solitude."

(3) Lastly, there is the danger of regarding contemplation as the whole of life. To commune with one's own soul, or with nature in her lovelier moods, and therewith to find God and to know his truth—this, according to the mystic, is to live. But to what end?—this is the final question. For life can justify itself, in the last analysis, only in self-forgetting action. Thus, contemplation, or inner spiritual communion, cannot be practiced for its own sake. As a generator of power, it must have an outlet. And what can this outlet be but power for use on behalf of men in their struggles for righteousness and peace. The mystic, that is to say, must be the most useful, and by no means the most useless of persons. I suppose the occidental can never adapt himself to the oriental attitude toward this question. The beggar in India, for example, on the highways or in the temple areas, seeking the support of offerings from passers-by while he spends his days in meditation! Or the saint who lives in seclusion through the year, and on one appointed day emerges to impart his wisdom to his disciples! Gandhi, a true Hindu, found the better way of linking meditation to action.

In our Western world, St. Francis of Assisi is the perfect example. So close was he to the common people of his time, so constant in his day-to-day, even hour-to-hour, service of their needs, so insistent upon the labor of himself and his brethren for the poor, the sick, and the distraught, that we are tempted to forget to include him among the immortal mystics of history. Yet his insight was so pure, his prayers so profound, his inner consciousness so intense, that in the end his flesh was marked by the stigmata as tokens of the spirit. No man came closer to God, or lived nearer to men.

V

Mysticism, in its true estate, is spiritual experience. It is therefore the beating heart of religion.

Reason at its best is the interpretation and formulation of this spiritual experience. Its product is theology.

Theology, like metaphysics, has its uses. One of these uses is not to serve as a substitute for religion. Yet the churches have persistently made this substitution and thereby wrought great ill.

There are many programs for the recovery of the churches. One assuredly is the rediscovery of mysticism. To supplant the theologian with the true mystic would save religion.

THE PROBLEM OF MYSTICISM

HENRY NELSON WIEMAN

THE MYSTICAL EXPERIENCE presents a problem which can be divided into four parts and put in the form of four questions: What is the state of consciousness called mystical? What understanding of this experience can be gained by psychological studies? What is the mystic experiencing when this state of consciousness occurs? What is the religious and moral significance of this experience?

I shall seek an answer to each of these questions by examining a number of studies [1] which have been made of mysticism. I shall also examine the experience portrayed by some of the existentialists to see how it is related to the mystical.

I am distinguishing one form of the mystical experience from the others because I think it is most significant. In a brief preliminary way it can be described as follows: There is first a breakdown of the protective devices by which the mind is shielded from sources of experience which cause acute disturbance. These protective devices are called "security operations" by Harry Stack Sullivan.[2] After this breakdown, or contemporary with it, occurs a

[1] Martin Buber, *I and Thou*, tr. Ronald Gregor Smith (Edinburgh, 1937); *Eclipse of God. Studies in the Relation between Religion and Philosophy* (New York, 1952); Albert Camus, *The Rebel* (New York, 1954); William Ernest Hocking, *The Meaning of God in Human Experience* (New Haven, 1912); Karl Jaspers, *The Way to Wisdom* (New Haven, 1954); *The Origin and Goal of History*, tr. Michael Bullock (New Haven, 1953); C. G. Jung, tr. R. F. C. Hull, *Answer to Job* (London, 1954); Erich Kahler, *The Tower and the Abyss* (New York, 1957); James H. Leuba, *The Psychology of Religious Mysticism* (New York, 1925); Jean-Paul Sartre, *Nausea*, tr. Lloyd Alexander (Norfolk, Conn., 1949); D. T. Suzuki, *Essays in Zen Buddhism,* Second Series (London, 1950); D. T. Suzuki, *An Introduction to Zen Buddhism* (London, 1949).

[2] Harry Stack Sullivan, *The Interpersonal Theory of Psychiatry*, eds. Helen Swick Perry and Mary Ladd Gawel (New York, 1953).

reorganization of the unconscious structure of the mind such that sources of experience can reach awareness which are profoundly satisfying even though they are integrated with what causes dread and acute anxiety when this integration is lacking. The wholeness of experience achieved by this integration neutralizes what was previously unendurable. "The whole idea" is the term used by Hocking [3] to designate this wholeness of experience. Karl Jaspers [4] calls it "The Comprehensive." This breakdown of the conventional structure of the mind and its reorganization in such a way as to render it more open to all which the human mind can experience enables the individual to find the whole of life satisfying, including what the existentialists call "the ultimate situations," such as death, guilt, chance, failure, suffering, and rejection.

A further consequence of this experience is that the total self approximates more nearly to wholeness in contrast to the conflicting parts of the total self which psychotherapy and clinical psychology have been describing at great length since Freud. Psychotherapy in its various forms tries to accomplish this transformation of the unconscious mechanisms which control what we shall perceive and how we perceive, what we shall dream and imagine and feel.[5] But psychotherapy does not attempt, nor could it achieve, any transformation of the total psyche so profound and radical as what happens in some instances of the mystical experience.

C. G. Jung [6] in his analysis and interpretation of the story of Job and the writings of Ezekiel, the Book of Revelation and other biblical writings, shows how those aspects of experience generally excluded from consciousness, which are terrifying, tend to reach conscious awareness as a consequence of the breakdown of "security operations" at the unconscious level. This represents one

[3] William Ernest Hocking, *The Meaning of God in Human Experience* (New Haven, 1912).

[4] Karl Jaspers, *The Way to Wisdom*, tr. Ralph Manheim (New Haven, 1954).

[5] See Frank H. George and Joseph H. Handlon, "A Language for Perceptual Analysis," *Psychological Review*, LXIV, No. 1 (1957).

[6] *Answer to Job, op. cit.*

stage in the development of the mystical experience. It is a stage which I am describing as breakdown, which may or may not be followed by the consummatory stage of higher integration. These most destructive and terrifying happenings first begin to reach consciousness in the form of symbols. These appear in the Book of Revelation, for example.

These visions of terror are symbols. They symbolize the dark and terrible aspects of experience which reach awareness when the protective devices of the unconscious are broken down and the more profoundly integrative powers have not transfused the darkness with light.

Before examining what others have said about this experience I shall submit an experience of my own. It may be diminutive in stature compared to the transformations recorded in the lives of the great mystics, but I think it has the same general character.

I

This experience was first recorded in *Religious Experience and Scientific Method,* my first book, appearing in 1926, although I did not in that account of it indicate that it was my own experience.

I had been separated from my wife and children for over a year. I felt under compulsion to continue my studies but must also support my family, and, if possible, have them with me instead of remaining where they were, halfway across the continent. I could do this only if I could get a certain kind of work that could be carried along with my studies. I made several attempts to get such work but failed. Finally, I received a tentative offer, providing I could make good. The first time I came I was very nervous, being worn with much study and having lived in much isolation in the attempt to complete the work for my degree. I did not do myself justice. I came a second time and at the close of the day was told that my employers were not satisfied with my services and that I could not have the position. It was nine o'clock at night at the time. I had to ride many hours on the interurban to reach my place of residence. I shall never forget that long ride of misery. It was after two o'clock a.m. when I got to bed. I could not sleep although I was worn with nervous strain, the day's work, and disappointment.

The hours of the night were almost unendurable. Worse than the disappointment and failure to find a means of seeing my family was the sense of my own worthlessness and futility. I felt completely beaten. It was total loss of self-confidence. It was not this last failure alone that overthrew me, but a series of experiences during the two previous years, which I had interpreted as failures. Because of these experiences I had been fighting the sense of failure and futility for some time. Now it rose up and crushed me quite completely . . . .

During the forenoon of the next day I attended to certain duties and in the afternoon returned to my room to face the facts as squarely and completely as possible and somehow find myself. I felt there was something must be fought out and settled, although I could not tell just exactly what it was. I suppose it was a vague sense that I must settle the problem of living my life and my relation to things in general. I felt there could be no rest for me until I settled things somehow.

I spent about four hours in my room alone. It was not exactly thinking, nor exactly praying, although at times it was one or another of these quite distinctly. Most of the time, I suppose, it was a sort of combination of these. Gradually there emerged within me a spreading sense of peace and rest. That almost unendurable pain of mind that had possessed me for twenty-four hours assuaged and passed away quite completely. I imagine it passed somewhat as a pain passes under an anesthetic. Then I found myself . . . almost laughing and crying with joy. Joy about what? I could not tell. I only knew my pain was gone, and I was full of great gladness, courage and peace. All the facts were exactly as they had been and I saw them more plainly than ever. My family was still as far away as ever and there was no visible means of getting them any closer. My failure to get the work I wanted stood as it had before. I cannot say that I had any anticipation of how my difficulties might be overcome. I did not even have the feeling that they would be overcome. I simply knew that I was glad, and ready and fit to go ahead and do whatever I might find to do and take the consequences whatever they might be. There was no hysteria and no hallucination about it. The strong emotion of gladness gradually passed away in the course of days, but the courage, peace, readiness to meet any fortune with equanimity, and joy in living did not go away. The old anguish did not return.

In the course of time I was able to have my family with me, but we spent the winter fighting to save the life of our youngest. For six weeks his life hung in the balance and for many days we had to watch over him constantly day and night. At one time he lay apparently dead and was only restored by artificial respiration. Yet through all this the old feeling of dejection and failure never recurred. Instead, a deep inner feeling of calm and divine presence was with me. In the years since then I have not kept to this high level, but I feel I have discovered the sources of infallible support in any time of need.[7]

There seems to be a level of being, or shall I call it a form of consciousness, which men can reach at times; and at this level all the dark realities of failure, rejection, guilt, unforeseeable catastrophe, while plainly seen and recognized in their true character, lose their power to darken the blessedness of life. What is this state of existence which human beings can sometimes reach? To my mind none of the traditional honorific titles apply to it—love, beauty, tenderness, truth, reality—none of these words conveys a meaning which properly characterizes this level and form of consciousness.

It seems that one cannot reach this state of mind until he recognizes in all their magnitude of evil what the existentialists are describing. Then, when the mind is purged of illusions and distractions and superficialities and becomes profoundly aware of its need, one may earnestly seek with the whole self until he finds this level of being where blessedness takes possession no matter what the evils. I do not myself understand this experience and am not satisfied with any of the traditional interpretations of it. The best I can do is to offer my own interpretation.

When all envisaged goods actual and possible seem as nothing compared to what the total self demands and seeks, and the apparent limitations of human existence seem unendurable, then the self can be liberated from preoccupation with achieved goods, subject as they are to destruction and impoverishment. When the self is thus liberated and in this condition seeks with uttermost self-giving to find what can make life livable, creativity can rise to dominance over anxiety and despair and all other concerns.

[7] Henry Nelson Wieman, *Religious Experience and Scientific Method* (New York, 1926), pp. 225-8. The experience here described occurred in 1916.

After using this experience of my own as an example of what I mean by mysticism, the studies which others have made of this experience will be examined, beginning with the work of D. T. Suzuki.

II

Suzuki has written very extensively of Zen Buddhism. While his language is different from the terms I have used to explain the mystical experience, what he says about it gives us a picture of Zen which seems to correspond to the picture of mysticism here under consideration. A few quotations from Suzuki's writings may make this plain.

> The individual shell in which my personality is so solidly encased explodes at the moment of sartori. Not, necessarily, that I get unified with a being greater than myself or absorbed in it, but that my individuality, which I found rigidly held together and definitely kept separate from other individual existences, becomes loosened somehow from its tightening grip and melts away into something indescribable, something which is of quite a different order from what I am accustomed to. The feeling that follows is that of a complete release or a complete rest—the feeling that one has arrived finally at the destination.[8]

> Ever since the unfoldment of consciousness we have been led to respond to the inner and outer conditions in a certain conceptual and analytical manner. The discipline of Zen consists in upsetting this groundwork once for all and reconstructing the old frame on an entirely new basis.[9]

> The main trouble with the human mind is that while it is capable of creating concepts in order to interpret reality it hypostatizes them and treats them as if they were real things. Not only that, the mind regards its self-constructed concepts as laws externally imposed upon reality, which has to obey them in order to unfold itself. This attitude or assumption on the part of the intellect helps the mind to handle nature for its own purposes, but the mind altogether misses the inner workings of life and consequently is utterly unable to understand it. . . . When we see a tree and call it a tree, we think

[8] D. T. Suzuki, *Essays in Zen Buddhism,* Second Series (London, 1950), pp. 31-32.

[9] Suzuki, *An Introduction to Zen Buddhism* (London, 1949), p. 95.

this sense experience is final; but in point of fact this sense experience is possible only when it is . . . subsumed under the concept "tree." *Tathatā* is what precedes this conceptualization; it is where we are even before we say it is or it is not. . . . There is a noetic element in *tathatā*. *Tathatā* is not just a poetic contemplation of, or an absorbing identification with, reality; there is an awareness in it . . . the whole is intuited together with its parts . . . the undifferentiated whole comes along with its infinitely differentiated, individualized parts. The whole is seen here differentiating itself in its parts, not in a pantheistic or immanentist way. The whole is not lost in its parts, nor does individuation lose sight of the whole.[10]

If I understand Suzuki aright he is saying that prior to the transformation of the mind which Zen calls *sartori,* yielding the experience of *tathatā,* the unconscious processes which determine what shall enter consciousness are molded by the practical and theoretical demands of daily life and the prevailing culture. As a consequence of this molding, we perceive and think and know by means of distinctions and structures which enable us to control and utilize whatever comes to consciousness. But when we do this, we exclude from consciousness the concrete individual wholeness of whatever concerns us, with all the qualities of sense and feeling which make up this wholeness. This wholeness is called tathatā, or suchness, when it reaches consciousness. The conventional mind, on the other hand, reduces everything to abstract forms, laws, and correlations which enable one to predict and control and reach some end which in turn becomes a means to some other end. But nowhere along the way do we find the concrete wholeness of sense qualities and feeling qualities which are in their wholeness profoundly satisfying. In science the abstract forms can be reduced in great part to mathematics. Whether with the precision of science or with the rough and ready pragmatism of daily life, these abstractions possess the mind to the exclusion of the concrete individual whole. Consequently we see a chair only with respect to those features which enable us to use it to support the body. So likewise with a tree or anything else. To be sure, the

[10] *Zen Buddhism: Selected Writings of D. T. Suzuki,* ed. William Barrett (Garden City, N. Y., 1956), pp. 269, 270, 272-3.

individuality with the qualities pertaining to it is not entirely excluded, but it is reduced to meager dimensions. With tathatā, on the other hand, the individuality of tree or chair or person comes much more fully to conscious awareness, with far more of its concrete, qualitative wholeness. Not only that, but what we might call the situation, which is more than any single object, reaches conscious awareness with whatever depth and fullness of quality the mind is able to experience after the transformation of sartori has occurred. And still further, this particular situation is not marked off from what existed before and will ensue in the future, but the present situation merges with the past and flows into the future with unbroken continuity.

The statement just made is misunderstood if it is thought that in Zen one experiences a Bergsonian flow of duration in which no objects are distinguished and no pragmatic structures are apprehended by which one can control and use distinguished objects. Rather, after the individual has attained sartori, which is the transformation accomplished by the methods of Zen, he does not cease to recognize objects and laws with all the distinctions and disjunctions required for this; but he experiences these as artifices superimposed upon the infinite depth and fullness of quality, and this "reality" gives to all that he experiences a value which is profoundly and continuously satisfying, no matter what may happen.

Prior to this transformation called sartori we encounter death, suffering, struggle, the sense of failure, unpredictable happenings which are disastrously frustrative and are called fate or chance. There is a sense in which all these "ultimate situations" occur in the lives of those who have undergone the transformation of sartori; but after the transformation the "ultimate situations" no longer convey the sense of disaster. Rather they are merged with the wholeness of life and thus acquire a depth and richness of felt quality which is "reality," profoundly appreciated as good.

What happens in Zen and in all the consummatory forms of mystical experience is a reversal in the order of evaluation of two things. The two things are: (1) abstract forms, structure, laws, distinctions, by which we exercise control and utilize the world round about us, including our own selves; and (2) the concrete whole-ness of the individual and the situation with all the qualities of sense and feeling which can enter into our experience of that in-dividual and situation. In the conventional mind, the pragmatic structures by which we exercise control are supremely important, while the qualities of sense and feeling are incidental appendages except when one indulges in "aesthetic experience" or contem-plates works of art.

The term "aesthetic experience" must be put in quotation marks, however, because that is not the experience sought in Zen, when "aesthetic experience" means a special kind of experience and not the continuous, most serious concern of everyday living. Zen experiences the wholeness of every object and situation and not merely those selected for their "aesthetic value." In Zen the qualities of reality are the continuous and most serious concern of everyday living. In contrast to these, the structures and laws by which we exercise control and utilize both self and things are rec-ognized to be artifices superimposed upon the infinite depth and fullness of "reality."

Thus it can be said that for the ordinary, untransformed mind, the qualities are incidental appendages while the pragmatic struc-tures of control and utilization are the important realities. For the transformed mind the pragmatic structures of control and utiliza-tion are the incidental appendages while the qualities of the whole situation are supremely important.

To the untransformed mind the statements just made about the mystic suggest either the aesthete or the self-indulgent sensualist because both of these give priority to qualities and second place to the structures of practical control. But this again is a misun-derstanding. The aesthete and the self-indulgent sensualist can find the satisfaction they seek only in certain kinds of qualities structured in certain definite forms. The aesthete must exclude the ugly, the trivial, and the boring. The self-indulgent sensualist must exclude suffering, struggle, and hardship. These are not ex-cluded in Zen but accepted along with all other "suchness" of reality, and this whole is found deeply satisfying. This does not mean that in Zen one prizes suffering, struggle, and hardship above other qualities. Rather, in Zen the mind is so transformed that one prizes the whole, that is to say, all the qualities which can be experienced in their unity to the limit of human capacity.

III

When we come to Martin Buber we find a metaphysic very different from that of Zen Buddhism and Hinduism. Buber is opposed to mysticism generally because mysticism is associated with a metaphysical theory which he rejects. Buber insists that his experience of I-Thou in opposition to I-It requires two persons confronting one another, each existing independently of the other. But when we examine the experience which he describes as I-Thou and see how he contrasts it with the common experience of I-It, we find that the experience, regardless of metaphysical theories, is very much the same as we have been describing as mystical, whether in Zen or elsewhere. It is an experience which casts off the protective devices and the abstract structures of pragmatic control and liberates the mind to apprehend the individual and the situation in their wholeness.

The I-It experience described by Buber is precisely that in which the pragmatic structures of control and utilization are dominant. In contrast, the I-Thou experience is one in which these structures cease to be important while the qualitative richness of the total concrete individual and situation floods conscious awareness. Furthermore, Buber has his experience of I-Thou not only in relation to other human beings but also in relation to a tree or anything else. When he has the I-Thou experience in dealing with a tree, it is, he says, the divine Thou which he is experiencing. But, he admits, this divine Thou is not a personality. God is not a personality but "loves as a personality and . . . wishes to be loved like a personality."[11]

I do not think that this dispute over metaphysical theory *about* the mystical experience should blind us to the likeness of the experience itself, whether found in Zen Buddhism, or in Buber, or

[11] Buber, *Eclipse of God* (New York, 1952), p. 81.

in some other. Buber does not claim to have any evidence for the divine Thou other than the experience of his own love when the I-Thou experience occurs. ". . . love itself bears witness to the existence of the Beloved."[12] But what is this love which he experiences when contemplating a tree? Is it not profound appreciative awareness of all the integrated qualities in that situation, made possible by liberating the total self from the domination of those structures which focus attention upon methods of control to the exclusion of the concrete whole? Furthermore, Buber's I-Thou attitude enables him to accept without despair the ultimate situations described by the existentialists—death, guilt, failure, chance, and other catastrophic encounters.

The Zen Buddhists deny that any divine Thou is involved in their experience of sartori; Martin Buber insists that there is a divine Thou. Thus they disagree in their metaphysical theory about the transformation which lifts man to a higher level of being. Both disagree in their metaphysics with Karl Jaspers, who is next to be considered. But the kind of transformation which they all proclaim, including Jaspers, seems to be much the same. All of them proclaim a transformation of the sort we have been describing.

In the following words Martin Buber defends his claim that a divine Thou is present in the experience of I-Thou.

> . . . we can glance up to God with our "mind's eye" . . . this glance . . . wholly unillusory . . . no other court in the world attests than that of faith. It is not to be proved; it is only to be experienced; man has experienced it.[13]

This claim made by Martin Buber calls for careful examination because it is often made in the name of religion and especially by the mystic.

Since Kant, the structure of knowledge has been studied very intensively to discover what knowledge is and how it is attained. The examination of knowledge in different cultures, analysis of the methods and achievements of science, observation of the way

[12] *Ibid.*, p. 84.
[13] *Ibid.*, p. 104.

the child acquires knowledge from early infancy, and description of the way we solve problems and get new knowledge in the daily experiences of life—all these studies have revealed one fact at least about knowledge. It is this: bare experience in its immediacy gives no knowledge. Some structure must be added to immediate experience and this structure must be tested through a sequence of occasions before we have any knowledge of what we are experiencing. This structure may be imposed upon the immediate data of experience as the result of a series of physiological reactions by which one learns to anticipate what will happen when certain reactions occur. This seems to be the way the infant acquires its first knowledge; and this process continues to play a part throughout life in getting the kind of knowledge called common sense. Learning the meaning and use of words, the formation of sentences, and thinking under the control of established structure of the language and of other symbols of the prevailing culture, all this is a further source of structures which can be applied to immediate experience in a way to yield knowledge. Still other structures are brought forth by creative imagination. When these are modified by proper tests they can be applied to immediate experience in a way to give us knowledge. From early childhood, and increasingly throughout the greater part of life, the individual acquires unconscious mechanisms which automatically apply certain structures to the data of experience so that we are conscious of little more than the structure itself, the data of immediate experience being in great part ignored.

When occasions arise bringing to awareness a flood of new data, the structures of knowledge may be submerged and lost in a flow of immediate experience. When no structure is applicable and testable in a way to give us knowledge, we may resort to noncognitive symbols and myths and aesthetic forms to apprehend this incomprehensible fullness of quality. Zen repudiates any attempt to comprehend this experience with the structures of the intellect.

If no structure now available to the human mind can be applied to this inchoate fullness of immediate experience in such a way as to give us knowledge of what we are experiencing, several alternatives are open. One may follow the example of Zen and not try to make any statement about it except to call it reality. Or one may do as Martin Buber and many Western mystics have done, namely, apply to this incomprehensible fullness of quality a structure of thought derived from Jewish-Christian theology. Still another alternative is represented by Karl Jaspers who says that this incomprehensible fullness of experienced quality is the Comprehensive.

By the Comprehensive Jaspers means the being which joins into unity the self and the object, or oneself and the other person. The untransformed mind does not recognize this unity although it is always present, says Jaspers. The conventional mind gives attention to the object or to the other person as beings which stand over against oneself, each existing independently of the other. Or, introspectively, one may examine oneself to the exclusion of other objects and persons. But in truth, says Jaspers, this seeming independence of self and other is an artifice set up for practical and theoretical purposes and almost universally practiced by the conventional mind.

When the individual undergoes what Jaspers calls "rebirth" he becomes conscious of this oneness, this wholeness, this Comprehensive, in which self and other are joined in one comprehensive being. This occurs when the protective devices fall away which exclude from awareness the "ultimate situations" such as death, failure, guilt, chance, and the like. Open awareness to these situations will drive either to despair or to "rebirth." This rebirth is a change of consciousness in which one becomes aware of the Comprehensive, and profoundly appreciative of it. The ultimate situations are then integrated into this wholeness so that one can accept them with equanimity. This seems to correspond to the experience sought and found in Zen Buddhism.

While Jaspers and Zen represent two different ways of interpreting the transformed consciousness, Martin Buber represents the third. He is typical of many Western mystics when they say that the great transformation gives them immediate knowledge of God. This claim need not cause dispute if it is clearly understood that "God," so used, is a symbol for a depth and wholeness of Being which no structure of knowledge can compass. But if these mystics mean to say that this experience gives them knowledge of God, as God has been theologically set forth in the Western tradition, they are making an indefensible statement. Sometimes they make the ambiguous affirmation that this knowledge of God is by faith. Such a claim only adds confusion. Either the experience gives knowledge of God or it does not. If it gives knowledge, the word "knowledge" should be used and not "faith."

The word "faith" and not "knowledge" is justified in this context if it means that "God" is used as a symbol to represent a creative transformation of human life which is of utmost importance, such as we have been describing. This symbol, "God," better than any other, may serve to indicate the supreme importance of this transformation. But the concept of God which may happen to possess the mind at the time one experiences this creative transformation is not knowledge derived from this experience. It is "faith" when faith means recognition of a reality which one does not understand but which transforms man to the highest level of his possible attainment.

Theology engages in a critical examination of religious beliefs, testing and reconstructing them, which may seem to be like the testing and reconstruction of theories leading to knowledge; but it is not. This theological reformulation of traditional religious beliefs is done to render these beliefs more effective in producing certain experiences and sustaining a way of life cherished in the religious tradition which is served by the theology in question. Beliefs treated in this way are an ideology; they are not knowledge.

So we conclude: when Martin Buber says that he has a certain kind of experience which he calls an I-Thou experience, in sharp contrast to I-It, there is every reason to believe that his account is authentic and altogether reliable. Furthermore, it seems to correspond to Zen and to what Karl Jaspers describes as the way to overcome despair when all defenses are down and the realities of life are fully accepted for what they are. But when Martin Buber says that his experience is the experience of God while the Zen Buddhist, who undergoes a similar experience, denies this, as Karl Jaspers does also, there is no way to settle the dispute until the concept of God is formulated in such a way that it is possible to test the truth of it by some kind of inquiry other than merely asserting it by faith.

IV

The existentialists are not, for the most part, mystics, certainly not in the sense in which mysticism is ordinarily understood. But the experience which they describe at length has a certain bearing on the mystical and for that reason helps the better to understand the kind of experience which we have been examining. We have already looked at Karl Jaspers, and a quotation from his writing will show how close he is to mysticism.

> I must die, I must suffer, I must struggle, I am subject to chance, I involve myself inexorably in guilt. We call these fundamental situations of our existence ultimate situations. That is to say, they are situations which we cannot evade or change. . . . In our day-to-day lives we often evade them, by closing our eyes and living as if they did not exist. We forget that we must die, forget our guilt, and forget that we are at the mercy of change. We face only concrete situations and master them for our profit, we react to them by planning and acting in the world, under the impulsion of our practical interests. But to ultimate situations we react either by obfuscation or, if we really apprehend them, by despair and rebirth; we become ourselves by a change in our consciousness of being.[14]

All the existentialists distinguish two kinds of situation. Jaspers distinguishes them here by calling one concrete and the other ultimate. The concrete situation corresponds to Buber's I-It situation and to the ordinary practical attitude which the Zen Buddhist contrasts with sartori. The ultimate situations, of which death and guilt and failure are typical, cannot be brought under control. We cannot treat them in the I-It relation. We cannot turn them to our profit. Therefore we must (1) keep them out of consciousness by unconscious "security operations," or (2) confront them in despair, or (3) undergo what Jaspers calls "a change in our consciousness of being," and this is rebirth.

The final consummation of human existence, according to Jas-

[14] Jaspers, *op. cit.*, p. 20.

pers, is not attained until one undergoes this change "in our consciousness of being" whereby we become aware and profoundly appreciative of the Comprehensive. As said before, this is a comprehending wholeness which unites self and world. To experience it richly and live in its power and keeping, the protective devices which exclude from consciousness the "ultimate situations" must be broken down and one must commit himself without reserve to this Comprehensive.

> Crucial for man is his attitude toward failure: whether it remains hidden from him and overwhelms him only objectively at the end or whether he perceives it unobscured as the constant limit of his existence; whether he snatches at fantastic solutions and consolations or faces it honestly, in silence before the unfathomable. The way in which man approaches his failure determines what he will become.
>
> In ultimate situations man either perceives nothingness or senses true being in spite of and above all ephemeral worldly existence. Even despair, by the very fact that it is possible in the world, points beyond the world.[15]

Here again we are told that there must be a breakdown of the inner defenses leading to the opening of awareness to the fullness and wholeness of being in which and by which we live. There may be considerable difference in what Zen Buddhism, Martin Buber, and Karl Jaspers say *about* this experience in terms of metaphysical theory but the substance of it seems to be much the same.

When we consider Albert Camus and Jean-Paul Sartre we find no mysticism; but their thinking helps to bring out the significance of the mystical experience because they have taken the first step toward it. They have cast off the security operations which conceal and deceive. Most of their work is devoted to denouncing and tearing away these evasions by which men deny and refuse to face up to what is truly involved in their lives. When we cease to cheat ourselves and to cheat life, when we have the courage to be honest, we see that the happenings of human existence are an "absurdity" and man must rebel against them.

One of the central teachings of Camus along with the other

[15] *Ibid.*, p. 23.

existentialists is that "man is the only creature who refuses to be what he is." This disposition of man has been developing through history, according to Camus. After tracing certain cultural changes which generate this view of man, he reaches the time of Hegel and Napoleon. This period initiates the more open and radical rebellion of man against his condition. Of this moment in history Camus writes:

> From this moment dates the idea . . . that man has not been endowed with a definitive human nature, that he is not a finished creation but an experiment of which he can be partly the creator.[16]

This idea stated by Camus is also proclaimed by Nietzsche, by Sartre, by Jaspers, by G. B. Shaw, by Erich Kahler, and by others: man is a being in process of creation through a series of transformations. Camus may not recognize mystical experience as the kind of transformation he has in mind, and many forms of mysticism are not. But there is a kind of mystical experience which is, and this we have been describing.

To awaken men to the absurdity of their lives is what Camus chiefly tries to do. It is also the main endeavor of other existentialists. This awakening requires the breakdown of the conventional mind. Whether the sense of "absurdity," "nausea," "meaninglessness," "guilt," and "despair" resulting from this breakdown can lead men to seek out and meet the conditions which must be present to pass beyond this state of mind and attain a more inclusive and meaningful integration of experience, is a question which only the future can answer. In any case existentialism is a first step toward such attainment because the breakdown of the conventional mind and acute discontent with man's present condition open the way to the further and more constructive transformation. When the constructive transformation comes to the individual rather suddenly it is a mystical experience of the kind we have been describing. If it develops gradually it does not appear to be mystical. Doubtless for some individuals, if it comes at all, it will be more sudden than for others.

Jean-Paul Sartre describes most vividly the breakdown of the

16 Camus, *op. cit.*, p. 106.

conventional mind. In his novel *Nausea* this disintegration of the conventional structures of conscious awareness is attributed to a fictitious character given the name of Antoine Roquentin. Roquentin has been looking at the root of a tree, at chairs, shoes, plants, people, all things visible at that time and place. The world around him no longer appears in the form of familiar, distinguishable objects. Everything seems to break down into an unstructured mass of immediate awareness which makes no sense at all. In the novel the experience is described thus:

> Had I dreamed of this enormous presence? It was there, in the garden, toppled down into the trees, all soft, sticky, soiling everything, all thick, a jelly. And I was inside, I with the garden. I was frightened, furious, I thought it was so stupid, so out of place, I hated this ignoble mess. Mounting up, mounting up as high as the sky, spilling over, filling everything with its gelatinous slither, I could see depths upon depths of it reaching far beyond the limits of the garden, the houses, and Bouville . . . I was nowhere, I was floating. I was not surprised, I knew it was the World, the naked World suddenly revealing itself, and I choked with rage at this gross, absurd being . . . I shouted "Filth! What rotten filth!" and shook myself to get rid of this sticky filth, but it held fast and there was too much, tons and tons of existence, endless: I stifled at the depths of this immense weariness.[17]

Erich Kahler interprets this experience of the existentialist, not only that of Sartre but of others also. The following is his account of it after very intensive study of its development and the social conditions which seem to have produced it.

> And then, getting down to the extreme bareness of existence, all these existences merge with existence as such, that common predicament of all and everything . . . that "paste of things." . . . Finally under the impact of all this tumult of amorphous existence, of constant suddenness, something happens like a revelation, like a mystical union, because the ego too gives in; the thinking, perceiving ego merges with the phenomenal mass of external existence. It is a mystical union, but by no means a mystical act. It is rather the opposite; a mystical giving in, a mystical breakdown. It is the last union of perception with the phenomena perceived, of the subject with the absolute. But it is a union that is not achieved through

---

[17] Sartre, *op. cit.*, pp. 180-1.

transport and ecstasy, through an effort of most intense concentration, as was the case with mystical movements of all times, but through *nausée,* through disgust. The absolute is not the supreme idea, not a supreme comprehensive meaning; it is the most dejected absurdity . . . the most abstract mysticism.[18]

Here we have the experience which ensues when the structure of perception and conception disintegrates, permitting the data of awareness to flood into consciousness without order, form, or meaning. What results is awareness of pure existentiality, "existence itself, something inexpressible, indescribable." This is mysticism at the first stage of transformation. It opens the way for a new and more profound integration, but the integration has not occurred. The integration waits on creation in the mind of forms of perception and conception which can give order and meaning to this mass of data.

The rational structures of Western culture, developed since the time of Greece and most intensively since the beginning of modern science and the Enlightenment, dominate the minds of the existentialists. These structures, developed to deal with the meager and highly selected data of science and other forms of efficient rationality, cannot be applied to the mass of qualities entering consciousness under the impact of the cultural conditions of our time. Especially is this true when one becomes acutely aware of the "ultimate situations" described by the existentialists. Consequently this flood of felt quality, breaking through the abstract forms of Western rationality, lacks structure, interpretation and integration, either perceptual or conceptual.

These experiences have been excluded from awareness in great part precisely because the highly refined abstractions of Western culture cannot interpret them in any meaningful way. But cultural conditions have developed of such sort that this mass of data can no longer be excluded.[19] When these experiences break into conscious awareness they lack structure and meaning not necessarily because it is impossible for the human mind ever to give them meaning, but because the abstract forms of perception and

[18] Kahler, *op. cit.,* pp. 180-2.
[19] See Kahler, *op. cit.,* for an account of these cultural developments.

conception developed in the West cannot be applied to them. But other forms of perception and conception can be, as shown by Zen Buddhism. The transformation in the organization of the human personality which we have been identifying with one kind of mystical experience is the acquisition of forms of thought, feeling, and perception by which this flood of data takes on positive significance and value. But until such forms of perception and interpretation are attained, the breakthrough of this unstructured flood of qualities must strike one as the existentialists represent it, namely, as "absurdity," "nausea," "meaninglessness." It causes "despair," to use the expression frequently employed by them.

The existentialists seem to assume that no forms of perception, feeling, and thought can be given to this breakthrough of experience because no forms fit to give integrative interpretation of it are available to them. They seem to assume that, since their minds and personalities as now organized cannot find any significance in this experience, therefore no human mind ever can. They conclude from this that existence is meaningless, absurd, and nauseating beyond redemption. But the interpretative structures of perception and reason available to the human mind are subject to radical and creative transformation. When and if the human mind undergoes the kind of transformation enabling it to acquire the forms fitted to integrate the mass of data given to experience by cultural changes now occurring, the absurdity can be transcended and a richer, more masterful life attained.

The religious existentialists, represented by Kierkegaard, Karl Barth, Marcel, Paul Tillich, Karl Jaspers, and Martin Buber, approach the breakdown of meaningful structure in the experience of modern life by a route different from that of the nonreligious existentialists. But they do not solve the problem as it must be solved if we are to undergo the transformation enabling us to comprehend the complexities of our existence in forms which not only satisfy but also are fit to give direction and control to our complex and dynamic civilization.

We have already looked briefly at the way Martin Buber deals with the problem presented by the existentialists. A glance at the procedure of Paul Tillich will further illustrate the methods of religious existentialism. Professor Tillich first exposes the mystery in which our total existence is involved. Then he employs traditional religious doctrines to serve as symbols and myths with which to give to this mystery whatever meaning the individual must have to provide him with the "courage to be." The courage to be, in this instance, is the ability to live effectively and devotedly, no matter how meaningless the actual events of our lives may be. Tillich's method for doing this is to find in the mystery the meaning which cannot be found by any intellectual understanding of the empirical world. He applies traditional religious beliefs to the mystery, not as true propositions, but as symbols pointing to something in the mystery which cannot be defined. This enables one to affirm beliefs about the mystery which seem to make one's life meaningful no matter how shattering the impact of death, guilt, failure, futility, and the other "ultimate situations" examined by the existentialists.

These beliefs about the mystery which enable us to endure the "anxiety" of our finitude cannot be asserted as knowledge, since the mystery cannot be penetrated by the human mind; but precisely because the mystery cannot be penetrated, the beliefs about it cannot be disconfirmed by contrary evidence. This is what Professor Tillich calls "beliefful realism." It also exemplifies his method of "correlation."

His method of correlation should be further explained. The two things which are correlated are: (1) human need revealed by giving full recognition to the lack of meaning in our lives and the other marks of man's finitude, and (2) religious doctrines about the mystery enabling us to derive from it what will meet this need. The correlation is between the human need which intellectual inquiry can expose but cannot satisfy and the religious doctrines which can satisfy the need by way of symbolism and mystery.

This method of the religious existentialists might be called a form of mysticism but it is not the mystical experience found in Zen Buddhism nor is it the kind defended throughout this writing. The mystical experience here defended is a transformation of the mind enabling it to find what satisfies human need in the everyday world of empirical fact and *not* by holding beliefs about a mystery beyond human understanding. The mysticism of belief about the mystery has been typical of much of Western mysticism. One should, however, distinguish between two things: (1) the psychological effects of belief derived from symbolism and mystery, and (2) a transformation of the rational structure of the mind enabling one to find life good even with full awareness of death and other marks of human finitude. The religious belief held by the mystic may symbolize the mystery, and the psychological effect of this belief may be the important thing for him. On the other hand, religious belief may symbolize not the transcendent mystery but rather a transformation of the total self such that one can find the great good of life not by looking to the mystery but by open awareness of each situation, including the ultimate situations.

The kind of mystical experience which is an actual transformation of the perceptual, conceptual, and feeling structure of the individual has religious significance different from the other kind of mysticism. The religious significance of this transformation is not that it points to a Being of mystery beyond the temporal world but rather points to a creativity operating in this temporal world, in the lives of individuals, in our interpersonal relations, in society, and history. This form of religion calls for ultimate commitment to this creativity.

One's whole life may be conducted in such a way as to be a symbol pointing in hope and faith to this creativity which, when required conditions are present, may transform human life to levels beyond our present imagining. This symbolism pointing not to a Being beyond time but to the creativity in time with its possible transformation of human life, is the most profound religious mysticism which can be lived. It can be lived because it can be the symbolism expressed in an entire life. The symbol is the life of the individual when this life is rendered symbolic by the way the individual conducts himself in dealing with death, failure, guilt, and uncontrollable catastrophe. This is the moral and religious significance of the mystical experience when it assumes the form of creative transformation.

ঙ৶ো IV ৷৹৵

THE PRACTICAL MYSTICISM OF
RALPH WALDO EMERSON

LESTER MONDALE

But the inner life sits at home, and does not learn to do things, nor value these feats at all. 'Tis a quiet, wise perception . . . we have powers, connections, children, reputations, professions; this makes no account of them all. It lives in the great present; it makes the present great. This tranquil, well-founded, wide-seeing soul is no express-rider, no attorney, no magistrate: it lies in the sun, and broods on the world. A person of this temper once said to a man of much activity, "I will pardon you that you do so much, and you me that I do nothing." And Euripides says that "Zeus hates busy-bodies and those who do too much."

EMERSON [1]

FEW IMPRESSIONS from Emerson's writings are so patently clear and unmistakable as this, that to him at least nothing could be more practically useful, from kitchen to studio and diplomatic conclave, than the ubiquitous transcendentalism of his lectures, essays, and poems. Here was none of the modest reticence of the mystic initiate before the as yet unilluminated. If the members either of the Mechanics' Apprentices' Library Association or of the Mercantile, the youthful Harvard Divinity School students and their hardly ductile instructors, the *Dial* subscriber, the Kansas farmer, the literary society, the Phi Beta Kappa Society sophisticate, or even Lincoln and his listening cabinet, were unilluminated, then it was imperative they were hearing the word. In the word was nothing occult or lolling or autistic, nothing transcending common psychological capacities. They, as he, might well be panning the auriferous flow of the Ethereal River. Therefore, neither occasion nor rank of hearer, nor the convention that de-

[1] Ralph Waldo Emerson, "Success," *Society and Solitude* (Boston, 1886), p. 293.

crees squeamishness, pianissimo at least, in the insinuation of religion into secular occasions, ever raised the finger of restraint to his utterances. As Dr. Jay William Hudson observed in his searching essay on "The Religion of Emerson":

> Religion permeated everything Emerson ever thought or did; it was not a function of his soul—it *was* his soul. Emerson was the sage essayist only as he was a religious sage, an orator only as he was a religious oracle, a philosopher only as he was a prophet, a poet only as he was a priest.[2]

His mysticism was not *mystic* in the ordinary connotation of the word—the ultimate in seizure and god-apprehension of the adept. What Emerson ceaselessly advocated was helpful, he assumed, equally to scholar, poet, artist, politician, businessman, housewife, philosopher, scientist, mechanic, public speaker, beleaguered parent, and preacher. This, despite his observation that

> the community in which we live will hardly bear to be told that every man should be open to ecstasy or a divine illumination, and his daily walk elevated by intercourse with the spiritual world.

His divinity, far from being fogged behind seven veils of Rosicrucian obscurity and centered in the inmost sphere of taboo and sanctity, was rather a hardy energy, equal to being described as *Father* in one mood, *principle* in another, and in yet another and without unction, *It*—an omnipotent force, met externally and internally, as rugged as the Andrew Jacksonite woodsman and pioneer, as common and yet as enigmatical as the dandelion, an omniscience as available to all and as essential to the chemistry of the mind as the gases of the atmosphere—like life itself, "dangerous and delicate." Acquainted at firsthand with divinity, as he knew it, one had the spiritual wherewithal to rise above the universal struggle for self-respect, a secure bunker against the batterings of untoward circumstances, a nonauthoritarian authority for ordinarily moot principles of right and wrong, as well as the means of achieving social justice at home and persistingly amicable relations abroad.

2 Jay William Hudson, "The Religion of Emerson," *The Sewanee Review,* XXVIII (April, 1920), 203.

Convincing as the practicality of this species of transcendentalism may have appeared to its proponent, it had by no means a like effect on his admirer and critic, Theodore Parker, ardently transcendentalist himself, who wrote:

> . . . he discourages hard and continuous thought, conscious modes of argument, of discipline . . . he exaggerates his idiosyncracy into a universal law. The method of nature is not ecstasy, but patient attention. Human nature avenges herself for the slight he puts on her, by the irregular and rambling character of his own productions. The vice appears more glaring in the Emersonidae, who have all the agony without the inspiration, who affect the unconscious, write even more ridiculous nonsense than their "genius" requires; are sometimes so childlike as to become mere babies, and seem to forget that the unconscious state is oftener below the conscious than above it, and that there is an ecstasy of folly as well as of good sense. . . . If Newton had never studied, it would be as easy for God to reveal the calculus to his dog Diamond as to Newton.[3]

To Horace Mann in 1837 Emerson apparently summed up the Commandments: "Sit aloof" and "Keep a diary." Earthy Carlyle complained in his letter of August 29, 1842:

> I love your *Dial,* and yet it is with a kind of shudder. You seem to me in danger of dividing yourselves from the Fact of this present Universe, in which alone, ugly as it is, can I find any anchorage, and soaring away after Ideas, Beliefs, Revelations, and such like,—into perilous altitudes, as I think; beyond the curve of perpetual frost, for one thing! . . . Surely I could wish you *returned* into your own poor nineteenth century, its follies and maladies, its blind or half-blind, but gigantic toilings, its laughter and its tears, and trying to evolve in some measure the hidden Godlike that lies in *it;*—that seems to me the kind of feat for literary men. Alas, it is so easy to screw one's self up into high and ever higher altitudes of Transcendentalism, and see nothing under one but the everlasting snows of Himalaya, the Earth shrinking to a Planet, and the indigo firmament sowing itself with daylight stars; easy for *you,* for me; but whither does it lead? I dread always, To inanity and mere injuring of the lungs! [4]

[3] Theodore Parker, *The American Scholar* (Boston, 1907), pp. 84, 85.

[4] Charles Eliot Norton (ed.), *The Correspondence of Thomas Carlyle and Ralph Waldo Emerson* (Boston, 1883), II, 11-12.

Labeling Emerson a "Western Gymnosophist" Carlyle wrote two years later:

> ... we find you ... a *soliloquizer* on the eternal mountaintops only, in vast solitudes where men and their affairs lie all hushed in a very dim remoteness; and only *the man* and the stars and the earth are visible,—whom, so fine a fellow seems he, we could perpetually punch into, and say, "Why won't you come and help us then? We have terrible need of one man like you down among us! It is cold and vacant up there; nothing paintable but rainbows and emotions; come down, and you shall do life-pictures, passions, facts,—which *transcend* all thought, and leave it stuttering and stammering! " [5]

The extent of the alleged unrealism, aloofness, and gymnosophism in Emerson demands, in view of the inability of the decades to pad him over beautifully with moss, a careful measuring. This measuring is best introduced by a few quotations which reflect in Emerson himself certain paradoxical character consequences that understandably mystified his critical friends. Parker, commenting on the literature in America that was written for something more than special occasions, wrote, "There is nothing American about it." But when he turned to Emerson he described him as "the most American of our writers. The idea of America . . . appears in him with great prominence." [6] How he could be the most American of our writers is perhaps suggested in George Eliot's observation in her diary: "He is the first *man* I have ever met." This happy personal embodiment of what is not only American in us, but also what is essentially human, was the comment recurrent over the decades since Carlyle, beginning with the words to his mother on young Emerson's first visit: "He seemed to be one of the most lovable creatures in himself we had ever looked on." [7] Quoting Harriet Martineau's reflection to his transatlantic friend, Carlyle wrote, "[she] tells me you 'are the only man in America.' " [8] Five years later (July 8, 1951): " 'Spite of

---

[5] *Ibid.,* p. 81.
[6] Parker, *op. cit.,* p. 62.
[7] Norton (ed.), *op. cit.,* I, 4.
[8] *Ibid.,* p. 113.

your many sins, you are among the most human of all the beings I know in the world. . . ."[9] On May 7, 1852:

> deep as is my dissent from your Gymnosophist view of Heaven and Earth, I find an agreement that swallows up all conceivable dissents; in the whole world I hardly get, to my spoken human word, any other word of response which is authentically *human*.[10]

The paradox of combining in himself a seeming hyper-Himalayan aloofness with that which is authentically American and human is heightened by the combination of this Olympian detachment with what is coming to be regarded as his profound immersion in the affairs of his day. True, he responded (Dec. 31, 1844) to Carlyle's Gymnosophist appellation with:

> what you say now and heretofore respecting the remoteness of my writing and thinking from real life, though I hear substantially the same criticism made by my countrymen, I do not know what it means. If I can at any time express the law and the ideal right, that should satisfy me without measuring the divergence from it of the last act of Congress.[11]

Nevertheless, as Harriet Martineau, who not infrequently came into contact with him on her 1835-6 visit to America, noted, prefacing her remark with this telling comment, "His home is the scene of his greatest acts":

> He is ready at every call of action. He lectures to the factory people at Lowell when they ask. He preaches when the opportunity is presented. He is known at every house along the road he travels to and from home by the words he has dropped and the deeds he has done. The little boy who carries wood for his household has been enlightened by him, and his most transient guests owe to him their experience of what the highest grace of domestic manners may be. He neglects no political duty, and is unmindful of nothing in the march of events which can affect the virtue and peace of men. While he is far above fretting himself because of evil-doers, he has ever ready his verdict for the right and his right hand for its champions.

[9] *Ibid.*, II, 195.
[10] *Ibid.*, II, 211-12.
[11] *Ibid.*, II, 85.

While apart from the passions of all controversies, he is ever present with their principles, declaring himself and taking his stand.[12]

The system of trade, *laissez faire*, he seems almost at times to identify with the Law of the Absolute; but then again, in *Man the Reformer*, with open eyes and clear conscience, "We eat and drink and wear perjury and fraud in a hundred commodities." A few more pages and he pins on the system these characterizations:

> a system of selfishness . . . a system of distrust . . . none feels himself accountable . . . no one feels himself called to act for man, but only as a fraction of man . . . The trail of the serpent reaches into all the lucrative professions and practices of man . . . Whilst another man has no land, my title to mine, your title to yours, is at once vitiated . . . We spend our incomes for paint and paper, for a hundred trifles, I know not what, and not for the things of a man. Our expense is almost all for conformity.[13]

Hissed at an antislavery meeting, deprived of lecture returns for some two years following the furor generated by his defense of John Brown, advocate of woman suffrage, friend and champion of the pillaged Cherokee—this believer in man as being at the moment the "soul now drunk with sleep . . . dwarf of himself . . ." this dreamer of the day when "we shall yet have a right work and kings for competitors," did not move through the scores of his years without having to mix with his daily drink no small potions of a hemlock that would try anyone's faith and serenity. Hardly in the class of the actionist ward heeler politically, or that of the Dorothy Dix campaigner, nevertheless he knew and felt what was going on, intimately and conscientiously, spoke his mind privately and publicly to eminent confidants. All of which more often than not constitutes social action that is effective and courageous as well as notable.

The impression he left with shrewd contemporaries of a cool, mountain-top detachment can hardly be gainsaid; and definitely misleading, as Parker justly intimated, are the vast claims of the

[12] Harriet Martineau, quoted in George Willis Cooke, *Ralph Waldo Emerson* (Boston, 1881), p. 103.

[13] Emerson, *Nature, Addresses, and Lectures* (Boston, 1884), pp. 222, 223, 224, 232.

Essays for the values of intuition. Nevertheless, there remains, mystifying but on further examination unassailable and convincing, the adamantine evidence upon which the Sage himself built his theory—the evidence of personal experience with its arresting day-by-day and over-all consequences in the integration and social-cosmic orientation of his psyche. In the sphere of the personal, within the cathedral-arcana of the locale of inspiration, nothing of science or ingenuity could have been more practically useful for the total Emerson. Why more men did not "cry with joy" over the "doctrine of this Supreme Presence," and thereby give birth to their genius as he did, was his perennial puzzlement. It was all so obvious to him; nothing supernormal, nothing in defiance of natural law, no "overpowering, excluding sanctity," but an experience as commonplace and universal as breathing, as secular as the psychology of reading or conversing. But quite apparently not so obvious to others!

Here in the man himself unquestionably is a "lost gold mine" lode worth digging for. Getting at it, however, calls for sinking more than one shaft through deposits of transcendental theory and the connotations of the terminologies of trance mysticism, Vedanta, and of the then conventional religion of respectable New England, in order to reach the very drifts he mined and the inexhaustible veins he felt he struck.

The cause for the misunderstanding of Emerson, we must hasten to add, lies not alone in his theorizing and terminology; and we offer the following merely by way of preface to the sinking of the aforementioned shafts. The difficulty of apprehension lies also with the reader, and particularly so in what a future age may well describe as the tragic flaw in the logic of our reasoning which all but excludes the intuitive. Intuition, exaggerated and by itself, we would grant with Parker, easily leads persons to "think themselves wise because they do not study, learned because they are ignorant of books, and inspired because they say what outrages common sense." [14] Nonetheless, the naive assumption of our era, that the whole is always equal to the sum of its parts, and that to grasp the whole—functioning man, mind, tree, or merely the in-

[14] Parker, *op. cit.,* p. 121.

organic "emergent"—is no more than a matter of investigating all
the facts of the constituent parts; this assumption can lead equally
to the opposite of wisdom, learning, and inspiration. Truth is
that the whole, any whole, physical, biological, sociological, is
always more than the sum of its parts. Therefore, without the
occasional leap of reason, the Emersonian oracular inspiration,
the metaphor transcending metaphor, symbol, and myth, our
minds stupefy for want of adequate self-understanding and we
perish for lack of the creative vision that persistently supplants
the ever-arising disillusion with the greater illusion. Emerson's
intuitionism as such, mystical though it be in context, can hardly
be regarded as a matter of inconsequence by an age which has so
recently seen entire nations go mad for want of an adequate dream
—not of bread, but of a humanly adequate adventure program to
go hungry for.

The heights of Emersonian intuition were far from being as
cool, factually vacuous, and breathless as they seemed to Carlyle
upon receipt of *Nature* and copies of the *Dial*. The genesis of
thought soaring from action and fact described by the early Emerson in 1837 before the Cambridge Phi Beta Kappa Society in
"The American Scholar" address is authentically autobiographical:

A strange process . . . this, by which experience is converted into
thought, as a mulberry leaf is converted into satin. The manufacture
goes forward at all hours.

The actions and events of our childhood and youth are now matters of calmest observation. They lie like fair pictures in the air.
Not so with our recent actions—with the business which we now
have in hand. On this we are quite unable to speculate. Our affec-
tions as yet circulate through it. We no more feel or know it than
we feel the feet, or the hand, or the brain of our body. The new deed
is yet a part of life—remains for a time immersed in our unconscious
life. In some contemplative hour it detaches itself from life like a
ripe fruit, to become a thought of the mind. Instantly it is raised,
transfigured; the corruptible has put on incorruption. Henceforth
it is an object of beauty, however base its origin and neighborhood.
Observe too the impossibility of antedating this act. In its grub
state, it cannot fly, it cannot shine, it is a dull grub. But suddenly,
without observation, the selfsame thing unfurls beautiful wings,
and is an angel of wisdom. So is there no fact, no event, in our

private history, which shall not, sooner or later, lose its adhesive, inert form, and astonish us by soaring from our body into the empyrean. Cradle and infancy, school and playground, the fear of boys, and dogs, and ferrules, the love of little maids and berries, and many another fact that once filled the whole sky, are gone already; friend and relative, profession and party, town and country, nation and world, must also soar and sing.[15]

Again, from the same source:

Life is our dictionary . . . I learn immediately from any speaker how much he has already lived, through the poverty or splendor of his speech . . . A great soul will be strong to live, as well as strong to think . . . the scholar loses no hour which the man lives.[16]

Several years later, he reassures the factualist Carlyle: "I only worship Eternal Buddh in the retirements and intermissions of Brahma."

All of Emerson's writings—which is also to say, all the enchantment and compass-point directives of his existence—are the end result of the "contemplative hour" during which the deed detaches itself like "ripe fruit" from life to become thought, a thing of beauty, transfigured. His is no piling up of synthetic judgments a priori. In this process of the deed, the grub, becoming the soaring angel of wisdom, is the autonomy of the ripening fruit, an evolution as much beyond the possibility of conscious motor control as heart peristalsis or the tides of metabolism. Here, then, was the high ground on which the man met his god—man full of life and living, looking on in the quiet of contemplation, while an awesome process, autonomous to his mind and will, transformed grub into that which had it in its power to soar majestically off into the empyrean. The man then was the deed, the Epictetus-like "spectator"; the process in man and yet more than man, creative and hence divine. Divine it doubtless might be termed; but not an enthroned Jehovah, not the revealing whisper for a Moses only, or a Christ, a select prophet; not an energy set apart by holiness and robe and chancel voice from the secular and from truth itself. Here in a sense was mysticism—not of the trance

15 Emerson, *op. cit.,* pp. 96-98.
16 *Ibid.,* pp. 98, 99, 100.

variety, but more in the form of a worldly daily habit of spectator contemplation which became a lifelong practice. The result
was neither the extreme of exultation, mystic union with oblivion,
nor the prolonged spells of mystic aridity, but rather an amazingly
sustained serenity that merited the adjective, beatific.

Grasping at an ideology that might best characterize and communicate the apperception at the heart of his literary creativity
and hence in his intuition of reality itself, Emerson identified
that which he regarded as the divine not only with the Absolute
of German idealism but also with the Ground of the medieval or
trance mystic, apparently also with the "tat Tvam asi" of Vedanta
lore, and then proceeded to elaborate in speech and essay in the
terminology familiar to those "with some religious culture."
Hence, culled at random from his letters and *Essays,* the several
connotations of his terms for the divine:

> Universal Being, Nature, soul of the whole, wise silence, universal
> beauty, primal mind, That Serene Power, truly human, one mind,
> aboriginal abyss of real Being, God is and all things are but
> shadows of him, that ineffable essence which we call spirit, the One,
> Universal Soul, Universal Mind, soul of all men, general mind, this
> deep of moral nature, mind of the mind, deep force, the nameless
> Thought, the nameless Power, super-personal Heart, majestic Pres-
> ence, other me, spiritual world, fountain of all good, supreme wis-
> dom, Intrinsic energy, pure omniscience, great reality, the Intel-
> lectual Law.

The immediate consequence of the several identifications of his
own experiential idea of the divine with the deity concepts of the
then-available ideologies led Emerson to excesses that give to too
many of his expressions an air of high romanticism, even anti-
nomianism at times, unreality, the impression on turning to one
of his essays of "going into a room highly charged with oxygen."
His Serene Power identified, or at least coalesced, with the Absolute of the Idealists, made necessary his transformation of nature
into the capitalized Nature of the Rousseauists, with a resultant
obliviousness to the machinations of the wasp laying its eggs in
the living spider and to those of the spider herself, that hardly
squares as it ought with the effects of overexposure to nature as

rightly observed, for instance, by Coleridge. His divinity, coter-
minous with the Absolute, becomes *ipso facto* omniscient and
omnipotent, with the inevitable corollary that he who realizes
God within takes on a priori a like omniscience and omnipotence, which is to say, genius: ". . . man has access to the entire
mind of the Creator. . . ."

That Emerson himself found, in his own impressions of the
idea-liberating process he observed in moments of contemplation,
facts that suggested omniscience and omnipotence, facts that
pointed toward the pretensions of trance mysticism, of Vedanta,
and of the religion of those with "some religious culture," is un-
deniable. The autonomy of the idea-evolving process lent itself
readily, all too readily, to ideological elaboration. Thus the problem for the modern reader is to disentangle the vaulting speculation from that which is valid deduction, from the essential facts,
from the psychological realities, of his inner behavior.

Looking on in the relaxed quiet of what is commonly described
as the first stage of mystic absorption, he noted soon enough and
with no small degree of accuracy that—

> We do not determine what we think. We only open our senses, clear
> away as we can all obstruction from the fact, and suffer the intellect
> to see. We have little control over our thoughts. We are the pris-
> oners of ideas.[17]

Along with this surrender to the idea-evolving process he also
noted, as will any who cultivate the art of relaxation, that he was
surrendering more than his mind, that he was the recipient of
more than ideas. The quiet of physical relaxation (if accompa-
nied by right mental attitudes) works with miraculous effect toward the easing if not actual removal of the anxieties that inhibit
the smooth functioning of physiologically autonomous processes,
and is felt as a refreshing and most effective energy. He correctly
and poetically infers from psychological fact:

> There is a principle which is the basis of things, which all speech
> aims to say, and all action to evolve, a simple, quiet, undescribed,

[17] Emerson, "Intellect," *Essays*, first series (Boston, 1888), p. 306.

undescribable presence, dwelling very peacefully in us, our rightful lord: we are not to do, but to let do; not to work, but to be worked upon.[18]

Give over to, give way, let go to this idea-energy process. Then, as he indicated in his famous passage in regard to his dealing with his intractable young son, one is greeted with an amazing social effect: "out of his young eyes looks the same soul; he reveres and loves with me."

What we have thus far denominated as the idea-energy process Emerson expands to further validly hypothetical dimensions. In his periodic surrenders of the ego—engrossed ordinarily in the universal struggle for self-respect—to the idea-energy process, he notes that the process functions apparently as a larger self with concerns markedly broader than eating, drinking, counting, and egoistic rivalries. But what in his own mind is the nature and extent of this seeming larger self is highly problematical. For purposes of communication it might be called Oversoul, God, Universal Being. But more accurately and factually described, "the divine, or, as some will say, the truly human, hovers, now seen, now unseen, before us."[19] Is it the divine, or more truly human—the Absolute, or the environmentally cultured and biologically inherited self of common humanity—to which he hearkens in repose? For public expression it may be the more theological entity; but this much he does know, as he stated in his "American Scholar" address in 1837, "there is One Man—present to all particular men only partially, or through one faculty; and that you must take the whole society to find the whole man." [20] Again, writing in the *Dial:*

Of the perception, now fast becoming a conscious fact,—that there is One Mind, and that all powers and privileges which lie in any, lie in all; that I, as a man, may claim and appropriate whatever of true and fair or good or strong has anywhere been exhibited; that Moses, Confucius, Montaigne, and Leibnitz are not so much indi-

18 Emerson, "Worship," *Conduct of Life* (Boston, 1886), p. 204.
19 *The Massachusetts Quarterly Review,* December, 1847.
20 Emerson, *Nature, Addresses, and Lectures,* p. 84.

viduals as they are parts of man and parts of me, and my intelligence proves them my own,—literature is far the best expression.[21]

Describing what may well have been the genesis of his developing speculations, the more mature Emerson wrote in the *North American Review*, April 1866, "Essay on Character":

Our first experiences in moral as in intellectual nature force us to discriminate a universal mind, identical in all men. Certain biases, talents, executive skills, are special to each individual; but the high, contemplative, all-commanding vision, the sense of Right and Wrong, is alike in all. Its attributes are self-existence, eternity, intuition, and command. It is the mind of the mind. We belong to it, not it to us. It is in all men, and constitutes them men.[22]

One further observation about the idea-energy process, then, is certain and factual, that in so far as it functions as a larger self it is also, regardless of whatever else it may be speculatively, an expression of the truly or universally human.

Individual man, so pathetically absorbed in pursuits that are calculated to enhance his uniqueness, and therefore respect in his own and neighbors' estimation, struggles on pointlessly and neurotically, oblivious of the larger context that, even in his fiercest efforts at exclusion and the enhancement of his uniqueness, he is naively advertising the Brahma-like dominance of the group. The greater his effort the more inevitable and greater his failure; and there is no ultimate gratification for the ego going in this direction, even when so expanded and so unique as to be in a position to boast: "I am the state." On this psychological pass Emerson commented in "The Sovereignty of Ethics":

Have you said to yourself ever: "I abdicate all choice, I see it is not for me to interfere. I see that I have been one of the crowd; that I have been a pitiful person, because I have wished to be my own master, and to dress and order my whole system of living. I thought I managed it very well. I see that my neighbors think so. I have heard prayers, I have prayed even, but I have never until now dreamed that this undertaking the entire management of my own affairs was

[21] Emerson, "The Senses and the Soul," *The Dial* (January, 1842), as quoted in George Willis Cooke, *Ralph Waldo Emerson*, pp. 217-18.
[22] Emerson, *Lectures and Biographical Sketches* (Boston, 1884), p. 95.

not commendable. I have never seen, until now, that it dwarfed me. I have not discovered, until this blessed ray flashed just now through my soul, that there dwelt any power in Nature that could relieve me of my load." [23]

Thus Emerson in yielding the ego with habitual regularity to the idea-energy-social process partook not a little of the rapture of the convert to the gentler and more humanely inclusive ethic, and of the rapture of the mystic. Continuing the foregoing:

What is this intoxicating sentiment that allies this scrap of dust to the whole of Nature and the whole of Fate,—that makes this doll a dweller in ages, mocker at times, able to spurn all outward advantages, peer and master of the elements? . . . I am representative of the whole; and the good of the whole, or what I call the right, makes me invulnerable.[24]

So much of a Platonic Good does he derive from his giving-over and the consequent openings, that he sees here compensation sufficient to counterbalance all conceivable personal suffering—the mystic solution to the problem of evil. Anent suffering he wrote to Carlyle (Feb. 29, 1844):

I have had happy hours enough in gazing from afar at the splendours of the Intellectual Law, to overpay me for any pains I know. Existence may go on to be better, and, if it have such insights, it never can be bad. You sometimes charge me with I know not what sky-blue, sky-void idealism. As far as it is a partiality, I fear I may be more deeply infected than you think me. I have very joyful dreams which I cannot bring to paper, much less to any approach to practice, and I blame myself not at all for my reveries, but that they have not yet got possession of my house and barn.[25]

These happy hours of which he writes suggest an antithetical and moot point in Emerson, his seeming high Puritanism in his elevation of moral law to the heights of divinity and its equation with God himself. This extreme moralism spoke the language of New England religion; in those environs it was probably an unavoidable verbal emphasis when coupled with an exegesis and

[23] Ibid., pp. 189, 190.
[24] Ibid., p. 190.
[25] Norton (ed.), op. cit., II, 59.

metaphysics so unconventional as to outrage the theological sensi-
bilities of Harvard Divinity School professors and the religious
populace. To such an eminence did he apparently elevate the
moral law that quotations taken out of the general context of the
basic facts of his artist-religiousness would appear to make him
somewhat antecedently an orthodox Ethical Culturist. The law,
on the contrary, is the basis of, the only context of, mental
predisposition upon which and with which one can make contact
with the God within, which is to be approached only by way of
the mind and flesh relaxed from ego pursuits. And relaxation, as
know all experienced in the art, admits of no relaxing away (by
physical effort alone) of the anxieties, tensions, functional dis-
orders that stem from egoistic mental attitudes to which one is
reluctant or unable to bid farewell. The law is thus implicit in
the experience. Hence, instead of Prussian-voiced, Kantian
capital-D'd Duty, one hears from Emerson: "The lessons of the
moral sentiment are, once for all, an emancipation from that
anxiety which takes the joy out of all life. It teaches a great
peace." [26] This same law operated with like effect in the relations
of man to man, he noted. It is the condition of any modicum of
satisfactory social intercourse:

> The least admixture of a lie—for example, the taint of vanity, the
> least attempt to make a good impression, a favorable appearance—
> will instantly vitiate the effect. But speak the truth, and all nature
> and all spirits help you with unexpected furtherance. . . . See again
> the perfection of the Law as it applies itself to the affections, and be-
> comes the law of society. As we are, so we associate. . . . . Thus of
> their own volition, souls proceed into heaven, into hell.[27]

Speaking in the same address of preaching as being the "expression of the moral sentiment in application to the duties of life,"
he goes on in the next sentence to describe the substance of that
preaching—thereby identifying the embodiment of the law with
contact with that which he regards as divinity:

[26] Emerson, "The Preacher," *Lectures and Biographical Sketches*, p. 216.
[27] Emerson, "Divinity School Address," *Nature, Addresses, and Lectures*,
p. 123.

In how many churches, by how many prophets, tell me, is man made sensible that he is an infinite Soul; that the earth and heavens are passing into his mind; that he is drinking forever the soul of God? [28]

To have a happy hour of gazing from afar at the splendors of the Intellectual Law, one must first—

disindividualize himself, be a man of no party and no manner and no age, but one through whom the soul of all men circulates, as the common air through the lungs.[29]

Again,

the law and the perception of the law are at last one; . . . only as much as the law enters us, becomes us, we are living men.[30]

Having received cornucopia graces in the form of an ever-astounding flow of oracular and soaring thoughts, like effects also in the form of regular accretions of rehabilitating energy, continuous psychic well-being, a remarkable realization in his person of an obviously lovable and common humanity—little wonder that Emerson moved unrestrainedly into the mythos of Idealism, Vedanta, trance mysticism, cultured conventional New England Christianity, and utilized without compunction and without discrimination their several doctrinal nomenclatures. Hence, of course, the omnipresent confusion in his utterances of *fact,* of firsthand practical mysticism, with *theory;* and hence, sequentially, the casually mingled earthy dews and damps with the angelically interplanetary ether of so much of his writing, the confusing conglomerates of shrewd common sense, seer and sage insights, with the excess of his mythos-premised unqualified assurances of compensation, self-reliance, revelation, genius, god-realization. Any study of this most American of Americans, this greatest of our dreamers of dreams and seers of visions, which mines to the living veins, to the metal of which his theoretical speculations are the dense penumbra, will find there the rich quartz of his strike. The student, moreover, will have before him

28 *Ibid.,* pp. 134-35.
29 Emerson, "Art," *Society and Solitude* (Boston, 1898), p. 51.
30 Emerson, *Lecture on the Times* (Boston, 1898), p. 274.

the splendid Emerson himself, exemplifying what this species of practical mysticism can mean (in addition to what has been suggested thus far in this chapter) in physical health, effective social rapport, aliveness to the supremacy and significance of the here and now (in contrast to the fossil-consolations of crystalline and dogmatic permanence), literary creativity, sympathetic humor, the cultivation of an authentic sense of at-homeness among men and in the universe, genuine *self*-realization, together with a lively sense of a vast, benevolent and ever-alluring potentiality at every turn of life's Chaucerian pilgrimage to some as-yet-to-be descried holy place.

✺ V ✺

MYSTICISM AND A. N. WHITEHEAD

EDWIN T. BUEHRER

Religion is the vision of something which stands beyond, behind, and within, the passing flux of immediate things; something which is real, and yet waiting to be realized; something which is a remote possibility, and yet the greatest of present facts; something that gives meaning to all that passes, and yet eludes apprehension; something whose possession is the final good, and yet is beyond all reach; something which is the ultimate ideal, and the hopeless quest.

A. N. WHITEHEAD [1]

IT IS ASTONISHING, when one thinks of it, that in a book such as this a contemporary scholar whose writings are to be explored for such insights as he may offer to a study of mysticism, should be a mathematician and a "secular" philosopher, rather than an accredited theologian or, let us say, a minister. It is hardly less astonishing to me that in all my reading and exploring of Whitehead's books I have yet to discover his first use of the word mystic, or mystical, or mysticism. The word itself seems entirely foreign to his vocabulary; and its omission from his writings could hardly have been an accident. Nevertheless, the inclusion of Alfred North Whitehead among those whose writings have inspired in the heart and mind of modern man thoughts and feelings generally recognized as mystical is obviously both necessary and significant; for it is impossible to read very deeply into his philosophical works, written during his teaching years at Harvard University, without being aware of the profound religious implications of his entire system of thought.

Basic to Whitehead's philosophy is his cosmology; and it is not too much to say that in the most profound and inclusive sense of the term all his philosophical thinking is also religious thinking.

[1] A. N. Whitehead, *Science and the Modern World* (New York, 1929), p. 275.

Throughout the pages of his books Whitehead haunts his readers with his constant awareness of the changing, expanding, creative natural world, and his sense of oneness with it. His philosophy gives expression to his lifelong effort to understand this together-ness scientifically, to grasp it intellectually, to feel it emotionally, and to describe it in language which can be understood. His was the receptive mind and the open heart; and perhaps more by him than by many a contemporary theologian have those who followed his thought during the past quarter century been moved to re-ligious contemplation. Despite Whitehead's complete omission of it from his writings, it is the word mystical, or mysticism, which one thinks of when one undertakes more clearly to charac-terize the religious faith of which he was the sponsor and the exemplar.

The cosmos is the setting and condition of all of Whitehead's intellectual probing; but following immediately upon his ac-ceptance of this primary fact is his poignant awareness of, as he likes to say, "the flux of experience." This phrase—and the prob-lems implied by it—is derived, of course, from his mathematical and scientific dealing with the problem of relativity; but in his system of thought it immediately becomes the dominating charac-teristic not merely of the universe objectively considered, but of all life. Whitehead's major philosophical work, *Process and Reality,* delineates the universe as a vast and inexhaustible plural-ism embodying an ever-changing, ever-moving diversity within the great cosmic unity—with every atom, every living creature, every solar system participating. It is this vast unity, or organism, en-folding this inexhaustible diversity—this endless creation and dissolution of entities within the whole—which constitutes the reality within which we live and move and have our being, and whose nature and destiny we share.

Here, then, is the clue to the religious insight and vision: reality is not just one (monism), nor a chaos of unrelated entities (extreme pluralism). Reality is the concretion of the many into what Whitehead ultimately refers to as organism, "the order of the world," "the ideal harmony." "The religious insight," says he, "is the grasp of this truth":

That the order of the world, the depth of reality of the world, the value of the world in its whole and in its parts, the beauty of the world, the zest of life, the peace of life, and the mastery of evil, are all bound together—not accidentally, but by reason of this truth: that the universe exhibits a creativity with infinite freedom, and a realm of forms with infinite possibilities; but that this creativity and these forms are together impotent to achieve actuality apart from the completed ideal harmony, which is God.[2]

Inescapably we find ourselves in what William James once called "a buzzing world," amid "a democracy of fellow creatures." These two related concepts—of togetherness, or organism; and process, or flux—need to be more closely examined. A phrase familiar to Whitehead's readers is *extensive continuum*. This extensive continuum "is one relational complex which underlies the world, past, present and future." Again,

An extensive continuum is a complex of entities united by the various allied relationships of whole to part, and of overlapping so as to possess common parts, and of contact, and of other relationships derived from these primary relationships. The notion of a "continuum" involves both the property of indefinite divisibility and the property of unbounded extension. There are always entities beyond entities, because nonentity is no boundary. This extensive continuum expresses the solidarity of all possible standpoints throughout the whole process of the world. It is not a fact prior to the world; it is the first determination of order—that is, of real potentiality—arising out of the general character of the world.[3]

Moreover,

. . . every entity is in its essence social and requires the society in order to exist. In fact, the society for each entity, actual or ideal, is the all inclusive universe, including its ideal forms.[4]

It is thus that the universe for Whitehead is a community into which all events and creatures are gathered, and to which they

[2] Whitehead, *Religion in the Making* (New York, 1926), pp. 119-20. An excellent discussion of Whitehead's conception of God and its divergence from traditional views may be found in William A. Christian, "Whitehead and Traditional Theology," *An Interpretation of Whitehead's Metaphysics* (New Haven, 1959), pp. 382-413.

[3] Whitehead, *Process and Reality* (New York, 1929), p. 103.

[4] Whitehead, *Religion in the Making*, p. 108.

belong; and the point of our discussion is that this fact needs to be emotionally as well as intellectually accepted. It is a temptation at this point to quote from two other intellectual giants of our time in support of this Whiteheadian concept. Albert Einstein is an unashamed mystic when he speaks of knowing "that what is impenetrable to us really exists," and manifests itself as the "highest wisdom and the most radiant beauty which our dull faculties can comprehend only in their most primitive forms"; and when he says that "this knowledge, this feeling is at the center of true religiousness." And as to Albert Schweitzer, his "reverence for life" is his intellectual and emotional acceptance of his fellowship with all living creatures.

It needs to be remembered that this togetherness, this sense of fellowship with the world of nature and the living creatures who with us share its destiny, is only a static, meaningless concept—forever beyond our awareness or experience—without the flux which is its very essence. There—everywhere—it is: this fundamental activity, this eternal movement and transfiguration. It is the unceasing movement of the planets and solar systems; it is the restless, driving energy within and around the atom; it is the eternal movement and change of wind and water: the rise of vapor into the skies, its drift with the wind across the continents, its distillation as rain and its transfer back into the ocean or up again into the sky. The flux of experience is the energy of the worker, the nervous striving and competing of the executive, the mental exertion of the scholar, the emotional ferment of the artist and the saint, the routine concern of the mother, the unfettered play of the child. It is the passage of the seasons, the endless stream of human events, the birth and growth and death and dissolution of every living creature. It is our human planning, purposing, loving, creating, and destroying.

The flux of experience is the fact that we find ourselves always, as it were, at the outer projection of passing time, constantly in the process of shaping and reshaping our lives into new structures and patterns of living. Every moment, every split second of passing time is pregnant with novelties of existence; and no event, no atomic entity, no living creature, no heavenly constellation, is ever excluded. All existence is gathered up in movement and change to which men and women must make their personal and social adjustment. With Professor Whitehead—following him, that is, through the difficult and intricate penetrations of his speculative mind—we come at last to feel this "welter of things," and we become, with him, conscious participants in the process—this eternal activity fashioning the self-transmitted past into some convergence, and ever merging into the future.

And be it noted that "the universe thus disclosed" is interdependent through and through. There is a coherence about the Whiteheadian concept which includes all, and from which nothing can ever escape or become lost. It is an "aesthetic grasping together," an "enfolding," rather, of countless concrete elements into a single unity. Here, then, is fellowship and participation on a cosmic scale; and failure to grasp the fact intellectually, or imaginatively, failure to make a full and free emotional response, is to miss the grandeur and the rich creative possibilities of the "event," which is our life within this welter of space-time.

So profound and total a grasp of the universe, of existence, of the reality, the process, which is the condition of our life—if pursued with intellectual and emotional eagerness—is bound to leave its impress upon the philosopher. It will make him, by virtue of his philosophy, a religious believer, a poet, and a mystic. Moreover, this sense of oneness, as we have already indicated, involves us unavoidably and—if we take our philosophy seriously—joyously, in an awareness of fellowship with all living creatures. Cosmic and natural mysticism, in other words, followed through to its logical implications, eventuates in social mysticism—the solidarity of the human family, the democracy of the races and peoples, shaping and sharing their common destiny. And inasmuch as every entity is in its essence social, and requires the society to exist—"an environment of friends"—the "Gospel of Force" must be replaced by the "Gospel of Love." Without some such transcendental aim—beyond man's present reach—civilization wallows in pleasure, or relapses into barren repetition and error. Nevertheless, "the aim at social harmony is plainly discernible as resident in nature."

Professor Whitehead's commanding religious vision, inscribed as a text at the head of this chapter, is therefore the logical and inevitable product of his philosophy. One must, of course, guard against a misuse of his words out of context, or a reading into them of one's own philosophical beliefs; but the text as quoted reveals as in a flash the heart of the philosopher's gospel and his faith. Here is the city of man's eternal dream: forever out of his reach, but forever inspiring him to new hope, new effort; and rewarding him with the varied and infinite possibilities of his striving.

> The immediate reaction of human nature to the religious vision is worship . . . The fact of the religious vision, and its history of persistent expansion, is our one ground for optimism. Apart from it, human life is a flash of occasional enjoyments lighting up a mass of pain and misery, a bagatelle of transient experience.
> The vision claims nothing but worship; and worship is a surrender to the claim for assimilation, urged with the motive force of mutual love.[5]

This mystic vision can be induced, invited, waited for; but it can never be forced. It never overrules, but it is always there, and it has "the power of love presenting the one purpose whose fulfillment is eternal harmony." Whitehead is not likely to be understood unless one is prepared to feel the deep spiritual quality, the emotional response which he unashamedly calls worship, and which overarches all his philosophical discussions; for, as he insists, "it is not true that we observe best when we are entirely devoid of emotion." Indeed, unless there is a direction of interest we do not observe at all.

The closing chapter in what some have regarded as his finest book, *Adventures of Ideas,* is significantly entitled "Peace." Having discussed many facets of his philosophy under such chapter headings as "The Humanitarian Ideal," "Aspects of Freedom," "Science and Philosophy," "Appearance and Reality," "Truth, Beauty and Adventure," he admits that "something is still lacking," apart from which the pursuit of Truth, Beauty, Adventure, and Art can still be ruthless, hard and cruel, and "lacking in some

[5] Whitehead, *Science and the Modern World,* p. 275.

essential quality of civilization." Pondering his problem, and rejecting such terms as "tenderness," "love," and "impersonality," he finally says, "I choose the term 'Peace' for that Harmony of Harmonies which calms destructive turbulence and completes civilization."

The "Peace" of which Professor Whitehead here speaks is not the negative conception of anesthesia. It is not a hope for the future, nor is it at this point concern for present details. It is, as he says, "a broadening of feeling due to the emergence of some deep metaphysical insight, unverbalized, and yet momentous in its coordination of values." And note: "Its first effect is the removal of the stress of acquisitive feeling arising from the soul's preoccupation with itself." Again, "there is thus involved a grasp of infinitude, an appeal beyond boundaries." Despite the sweep and grandeur of such a vision—or shall we not say, because of it? —Whitehead's utter philosophical and religious candor forces upon him the conclusion that life is ultimately tragic. The essence of nature is flux—concretion and disintegration—birth, growth, death, and dissolution. Always we have the "dream of youth and the harvest of tragedy." The experience and the meaning of peace is therefore to be understood only as we consider it in its relation to the tragic issues which are unavoidable—nay, essential—in the nature of things. Tragedy is the price we pay for our existence, for adventure in living. There can be no peace save through the understanding of tragedy, and—paradoxical though it may seem —through the understanding of it we guarantee its preservation. In a sense, too, the experience of peace is largely beyond the control of purpose or conscious striving. It comes as a gift; the deliberate "aim at Peace" very easily passes into its "bastard substitute," anesthesia. The peace of which Professor Whitehead speaks is not unlike Wordsworth's

> . . . sense sublime
> Of something far more deeply interfused,
> Whose dwelling is the light of setting suns.

Whitehead himself, more perhaps than Einstein and Schweitzer, is living evidence that the mystic experience—the experience, namely, that there is in nature a reality akin to ourselves—need not be foreign to men of great intellect, great power, and unbelievable capacity for sustained activity. The mystics of history are a great company. Consider John Scotus Erigena, and Nicholas of Cusa, and Bruno, and Jacob Boehme, and Spinoza. The mystic is a radical, and whatever divergent religious beliefs or practices may distinguish him from his fellow men he is without caution or compromise in his assertion of the essential worth of life. Mysticism is therefore a road which naturalists and humanists may themselves travel. It could, of course, lead to escape from the world, and often does; but even such Christian mystics as Saint Teresa and Saint Francis and George Fox labored tirelessly, and with courage almost unsurpassed. Professor Hocking once said that it may be wondered whether any great reform has ever occurred in history without some mystic at the bottom of it; nor is it difficult to understand how the qualities of moral courage are peculiarly associated with mysticism.[6]

Again, mystics have been unremitting in their effort to understand and to express what to them is always the inexpressible. Pascal observed that "the heart has reasons that reason cannot know," but it can hardly be said that Pascal shrank from the discipline of reason. And Whitehead, often chafing under the frustrations and limitations of language to express logical or descriptive thought, said that "mothers can ponder many things in their hearts which their lips cannot express." Nevertheless, said he:

> It is not the case . . . that our apprehension of a general truth is dependent upon its accurate verbal expression. For it would follow that we could never be dissatisfied with the verbal expression of something that we had never apprehended.[7]

---

[6] "This masterful attitude toward types of conduct which have the name of virtue fits the mystic to be a moral originator, a reformer of laws and customs. He has so often filled this role that it would be interesting to enquire whether any great reform had occurred in history without some mystic at the bottom of it." William Ernest Hocking, *Types of Philosophy* (New York, 1959), p. 271.

[7] Whitehead, *Religion in the Making*, p. 126.

In summary, it could be contended that cosmic (or naturalistic) and social mysticism are the logical and necessary expression of those who find themselves in general agreement with Whitehead's philosophy of organism even if they remain unmoved by his development of the concept of God. For Whitehead "the purpose of God is the attainment of value in the temporal world." In associating the concept of God with the search for values Whitehead nowhere makes the claim that the universe guarantees values, or the achievement of moral character. What he does claim is that religious truth "brings to our consciousness that permanent side of the universe which we can care for." It thereby provides a meaning in terms of value for our own existence, a meaning which "flows from the nature of things." The new insights emerging today in the best of our art, our literature, our science, our philosophy, our political ideals, and our evolving concepts of human rights, are indications of a creative process which though "secular" is nevertheless religious. Thus we learn that we must discover the holy in that which, instead of denying those insights or minimizing their worth, brings them into a new and working synthesis.

Here, then, is possible a mystical experience of a high order, for which we can find support in "secular" philosophy, in the scientific probing of an Einstein, or in the humane service of a Gandhi or a Schweitzer. It is the kind of mysticism which will in the future draw heavily upon the logical mind and the metaphysical insight of Alfred North Whitehead. In the solution of our human problems we need Whitehead's far-ranging sweep of our cosmic setting, for increasingly the co-operative venture of mankind will need to enlist the mystical adherence of all men of good will. And, as Irwin Edman once said,

> social institutions will be the sacraments of that Beloved Community in which all men are brothers.

Reference has been made to the moral courage of the great mystics of history. The mystic experience has for its function the recovery of freedom as well as the search for value; and what the mystic stands to gain from his vision and his self-discipline is inner certainty, stability of character, moral invulnerability, serenity, and peace. In the light of such testimony from history, added to the philosophical support which we find in Professor Whitehead, this discussion would be incomplete without a footnote on the personal character of the philosopher. Those who studied under Whitehead at Harvard speak of his unforgettable face, his smile, his voice,

> the humanity, the kindness, the understanding, the tenderness and the living humor of the man.[8]

They bear testimony to his inward calm, his complete absence of dogmatism, his "childlike tentativeness," his utter, human goodness. Whitehead knew that the contemporary philosophical trend, as exemplified, for example, in the philosophies of Bergson, William James, and even John Dewey, suffered from the charge of anti-intellectualism. Into this philosophical ferment he brought his logical, mathematical mind, intent on rescuing their type of thought from the charge rightly or wrongly attached to it.

Meanwhile, it is his rigid logic, his speculative and imaginative mind, his unfettered naturalism, and his unashamed emotional outgiving which we need to rescue liberal religion from the hesitancy and confusion in which it is floundering. Devoid of the ancient substructure of the Christian doctrine of sin and the traditional techniques of salvation, liberal religion has lacked the incentive to take its intellectual and social responsibility seriously; and it has usually been too respectable to really give itself to a profound and uninhibited emotional expression. We have hesitated at the crucial point, hoping somehow to keep within sight of the lighthouse of Christian faith, but being yet somewhat ashamed of the emotional response necessary to keep alive the glow and the zest of the religious spirit.

Professor Whitehead did not hesitate. He bade us set sail on the great cosmic adventure—boldly, unafraid. What is there to fear? Cosmic tragedy? Perhaps, at last! The ultimate dissolution of human existence on earth? That too, perhaps. But even this tragedy, as Whitehead suggests, can be clothed and perceived as Beauty;

[8] See Charles Malik, "An Appreciation of Professor Whitehead, with Special Reference to his Metaphysics and to his Ethical and Educational Significance," *The Journal of Philosophy*, XLV, 21 (October 7, 1948), 572-82.

for even if it eventuates it cannot destroy the zest of the experience of living and understanding and feeling which today is ours. Meanwhile, "since life is good, let men be good," and with Tennyson's *Ulysses*—as with Whitehead—we may experience the great ongoing:

> . . . Come, my friends,
> 'Tis not too late to seek a newer world.
> Push off, and sitting well in order smite
> The sounding furrows; for my purpose holds
> To sail beyond the sunset, and the baths
> Of all the western stars, until I die.
> . . . that which we are, we are,—
> One equal temper of heroic hearts,
> Made weak by time and fate, but strong in will
> To strive, to seek, to find, and not to yield.

MYSTICISM AND NATURALISTIC HUMANISM

KENNETH L. PATTON

Doubtless there is a Mystery, but it does not stigmatize reality; the mystery is on our side of the fact. Despite Schwegler's "certain existent unreason," it were the height of presumption on our part to proclaim the ultimate surd. The factual world needs no accounting for, *in itself,* as we need for it. We are late, we are ephemeral, and mainly inconsequent; yet the fact that the mystery is in our own incompetence only lends dignity and charm to its revelation, and into our initiation into a prestige supremely worth while.

BENJAMIN PAUL BLOOD [1]

IN RELIGION a man seeks the deepest knowledge and wisdom of which he is capable. He stands before the fact of his own existence, amid the turbulence of his associations with his fellow men, faced with the infinities of time and space in the surrounding universe, and attempts to assess the measure and meaning of his brief existence. Whether his answers are confident or ridden with questions and mystery depends on his assurance as to the adequacy of his own insights and his faith in the savants and scriptures to which he turns for authority. It would seem fair to judge that all men face this problem with roughly the same equipment of senses and thought. Some are more perceptive and intelligent than others, but to believe that some few are equipped in so extraordinary a manner as to set them quite apart from other men as receivers of a unique revelation would seem not to be proven by adequate evidence. Our studies of human history reveal all men as the products of the opportunities and limitations of their own day. And search as we may, we find none of our contemporaries confounding us with signs of superhuman powers.

[1] Benjamin Paul Blood, *Pluriverse, an Essay in the Philosophy of Pluralism* (Boston, 1920), p. 238.

But this is not the opinion of everyone. Mankind is divided into two schools on this matter. There are those, myself included, who believe that all men are equally natural and human creatures, with faculties limited to the senses and thinking functions of their organisms, which garner and work upon experiences in a world that is available in commonalty to all men. All men are physical creatures with a delicate and responsive nervous system which differs only in subtlety and complexity from the nervous systems of other animal life. There is another school which claims to find, in addition to this physical nature of man, what it calls man's spiritual nature. This spiritual nature has its own windows and its own wisdom, so they say. In addition to the senses of the body, there are the eyes and the ears of the soul. This higher awareness and wisdom they have called "mysticism."

There is one essential difference between the two fields of experience and knowledge in this second school of thought. The one way of knowing, the physical, is open to all men through their senses and their reason. But the other experience is inner, unsharable, and beyond defining and reporting in words. There is no way that this kind of evidence and assurance can be shared or checked. It is either known self-evidentially or it is not known. Those who share these faculties and experiences hold a common conviction as to the validity of their mystical revelations. Those who are outside the esoteric fold may either lament their obtuseness and limitations, or else be convinced that the mystics delude themselves. The latter may be perfectly sincere in stating that they have felt certain things, but the skeptics are doubtful that they have made legitimate deductions from their experiences.

The judgment as to the nature of human experience, whether it is of one kind alone, physical and material, or whether it is of two kinds, also spiritual, rests upon a deeper assumption regarding the nature of the universe itself. Is the universe all physical and natural, or are there two realms of being, the material and the spiritual? The assumption that some men are equipped with mystical powers whereby they can perceive spiritual truths assumes that such a wider spiritual realm exists from which the truths can emanate. It is evident that whichever assumption a person makes, he is a creature like to all other men, and exists in the same world with all other men. To believe or disbelieve in one of these theories would not change his nature. He would be likely to have experiences similar to those of his fellows, and differ from them chiefly in the interpretations he placed upon his experiences.

The interpretation of the universe, and the interpretation of human experience by those who believe in the spiritual realm, has been adequately set forth by those who are convinced of its reality. Those who have had no "spiritual" experiences, and who doubt this interpretation of the world and man, have no right and no ability to judge upon its existence or nonexistence. Here they can be none else than agnostic. They may, if they choose, be deeply skeptical. They may offer substitute explanations for those experiences that others call spiritual. They may be convinced that they have had the same, or similar, experiences, and that these are capable of explanation in natural terms. If this is so, they can attempt an explanation of those experiences called spiritual and mystical, and describe the wealth of satisfaction and insight which they bring to one who believes himself fully encompassed within one, continuous, natural world. They must rest their case on the adequacy of their own interpretation, for the field of those with the other opinion is by definition closed to them. To one who believes in the two realms, an explanation of life and man in terms of one realm may seem meager and stultifying. The only answer is that expanse and splendor have little to do with number of realms. One room can be larger than two smaller rooms together. In qualitative terms, the material realm may come to appear so abounding in variety, subtlety, beauty, depth, and mystery that it will include within it the qualities of existence and experience that once were thought to belong to a spiritual realm, and the materialist will feel that he has canceled out nothing of reality and possibility in postulating a universe of one stuff and extension.

Within this single and continuous environment it may be possible to identify certain experiences which in their intensity and rarity seem to stand apart from the daily course of events. Herein

one may feel himself to have been unusually acute and perceptive, to have seen more largely and deeply into the meaning of
things than at other times. He may borrow a term from the other
school, and say that these are mystical experiences. He may sur-
mise that the other parties, struck by the awesome intensity of
such moments, have sought to explain them by referring them to
a superior realm. Sympathetic as he may be to this judgment,
knowing his own baffling sense of mystery and transport, he will
yet feel that great harm is done by splitting nature and man into
two components in order to explain depth and variety of experience. If he uses the term mysticism, he does so to describe a quality
of experience, not to define that experience as distinct and separate from other experiences. He uses the word as he would use
the words dull and sensitive, gay and sorrowful.

What is the interpretation of man that the naturalist assumes
when he includes mystical experiences as in no essential way
different from any other experiences? A man is seen to be in kind
like to all other natural things. He partakes of the activity and
irritability of all matter. To him all matter is made of energy and
is, except at extremely cold temperatures, in a state of almost incredible activity. He has been told by the scientists that, instead of
being solid as it sometimes seems, it is in its microcosmic dimensions so sparse as to seem almost immaterial. It ceases, almost, to
have body and to resemble more light and electricity, which he
has been wont to use as descriptive symbols for spirit in other
times. He has been accustomed to think of living creatures as
things capable of self-movement, but he learns that the smallest
components of matter are in a constant self-movement so swift
that it makes the gross movement of a living creature seem almost
inert.

He also learns that all matter responds to other matter within
its environment. In fact, the physicists are lately talking about
matter itself as fields of force, in which each field of force extends
into and through the neighboring field of force, just as the light
of one candle will shine through the light of other candles near-
by. In fact, Whitehead says that every atom prehends, or is in

relation to, every atom in the universe. These microcosms collide with one another, attract or repel one another, unite and separate, invade one another. All things, living and dead, are in responsiveness and interchange. And the categories that once held uniqueness for living creatures now become inclusive of everything.

It is the way of the material of nature to be in constant flux, to be combining into ever more complex molecules, cells, organs, and organisms, and to be separating and breaking up, only to recombine in other temporary and shifting wholes. These larger wholes, made of incomprehensible numbers of microcosms, are themselves in more or less sensitive relationship to surrounding objects. Even the stones react to the air, earth and sun, and living creatures. A human being is in no essential way different in his response to his environment from any other material object or creature. True, he has his own varieties of responses, but they are only extensions and proliferations of kindred responses observed in other creatures.

In one of the smallest forms of living creature, the amoeba, we observe a certain irritability, a sensitiveness to light and to heat and cold, and a reaction to foreign objects as food. As we go up the scale of specialization and complexity in living creatures, we find the more general irritabilities and responses of the amoeba becoming specialized into sense organs of feeling, seeing, hearing, tasting, smelling, and the many other types of sensual response. The creatures also develop various means of responding to outside stimuli in terms of locomotion, combat, eating, temperature control, communication, all the endless activities of life. Although man in his total response and activity seems to be more subtle and complex than any other creature, in many specific senses and abilities he falls far short of some of his fellow denizens of the earth. He has not the eye of the eagle and the fly, nor the delicate nose of the dog and the deer, nor the touch of the insect's antenna, nor the delicate ear of the bird, nor the strength of the gorilla and elephant, nor the speed of the greyhound and cheetah. In skeleton, musculature, organs, nervous system, brain structure, he bears close family resemblance to the other mammals. Other creatures have organs of speech, intelligence, and perhaps even a rudimentary ability to handle abstract symbols, and to think.

The naturalist or materialist includes man with all the other things and creatures of nature. He adds to him no special "spiritual" faculties by which to explain those further extensions of activity that differentiate man from his fellow creatures. He endows man with no "soul," nor with spiritual faculties. He attempts to explain man in all his complexity in sensual, emotional, rational, and intuitional terms. Man, like the amoeba, is irritated by things about him and reacts to them. Added to his reactions to his external environment he has reactions to his internal environment, the sensations of the viscera, hunger, nausea, dizziness, pain, fatigue, elation, depression, doubt, fear, anger, confidence. Just as the air is constantly entering him and being expelled, so the outside impinges upon him and enters him, and he in turn acts as an object in the environment of others.

There was a time when that line of evolutionary development which produced man exhibited no creature with man's distinctive attributes. No animal used words and thought with the use of symbols and structures of rhetoric and logic. No animal made and used tools and gadgets. But somewhere grunts became differentiated to stand for different objects and experiences, speech developed, the wordless memory of the animal acquired the implementation of symbols and thought patterns, and in time was supplemented by writing and records.

The essential problem that faces man arises from the confusion added to his nature when the ability of speech and thought and culture building was added to the body which for millions of years had been conditioned to respond instinctively to the emergencies and necessities of existence. New ranges of confusion and enlightenment, joy and agony, virtue and vice, success and failure were opened to this creature. The simplicity of life, the untroubled animal acceptance and contentment in existence were forever lost to him. And man sought to find on another level, the level of thought and understanding, that relationship to the world about him which had become so badly confused and perverted.

Much as man depends on the response of the world outside himself for the experiences and sensations whereby he acquaints himself with the world and arrives at understanding, he is peculiarly dependent upon his own nature. All other animals live in the same world as he, but only man arrives at understanding, at artistic appreciation, at philosophic wisdom, at religious exaltation. In this sense man is not dependent upon revelation from outside himself, but rather upon his own senses and rational processes and emotional reactions. He reacts to the universe always in the terms and limitations imposed by his human nature.

This human nature is never a fixed entity. Each person has an individual constituency of sense perceptions and acuity, of intellectual keenness with which to relate and assemble his experience, and a store of memories and judgments whereby experiences are conditioned and interpreted. Each person is never for two moments the same person, as his accumulation of experience enlarges, as the tone and responsiveness of his body changes, as his attention shifts and his concentration varies. His digestion, glands, state of health, comfort, all affect his awareness and mood of appreciation. The mature person becomes an incredibly complex system of memories, habits, aversions, anticipations, sensitivities, stupidities, and wisdoms. He is capable of reacting in limitless variations as differing patterns of reactions assert themselves.

Sometimes the line of association and reaction seems commonplace. We eat a slice of bread, walk down a familiar street, see a well-known face, read a previously known opinion, and we are undisturbed in our easy acceptance of the accustomed routine of experience. We are not even conscious of novelty, but rather of the recurrence of the expected. If the routine is habitual enough, these happenings may not even be consciously noted. We are consciously aware of only a fraction of what we do and of what goes on around us. Usually we concentrate on one line of activity or observation at a time—the book we are reading, the voice to which we are listening, the idea of our contemplation. Such times do not disturb us, or shock us with some unaccustomed meaning or insight, or acute reaction or emotion. Occasionally experiences hardly noted in such torpid moods will be recalled later and evidence an unwarranted significance which we did not recognize earlier.

There are other times when we are more alert, when something new is happening, when our interest is sharp, and we feel that new comprehensions are breaking open within us. There are similar times when a drama, a piece of music, a conversation, playing a game, love-making, an absorbing piece of work, will completely hold and entrance us. In such moments we are not critical or even self-conscious, and yet grandly alive. We look back upon such states as conditions of happiness.

But there is yet another kind of experience which I would call mystical, and which is perhaps of the same quality that others might interpret as spiritual and as providing contact with and knowledge of a realm above the physical, mundane order of everyday life. It comes in many forms, but has the common property of etching experience in a new clarity, a greater significance, a further penetration of meaning than we have known before. Perhaps this is why some credit it to the visitation of a power from above and the revelation of truth from a supernatural and perfect being.

There are moments when the sheerest and simplest sensual experience wears a golden significance. Suddenly, as the atmosphere is crystal clear after a rain, objects take on a naked, transparent meaning. We are probed and wounded by the smooth, chill surface of glass, by a flashing sword of color, by the explosive individuality of a bird or a child. We are stabbed by the isness, the thatness of things, and there comes a fresh and splendid sense of existence. These experiences differ from those in which we become absorbed, in that they shock us into self-awareness, as we are sharply moved to acknowledge the individuality, the shattering presence of something outside ourselves.

In these moments objects seem to be revealed to us in a new clarity and fineness. It is as if we had seen only one side of a statue, and then suddenly come upon it in the round, and could see it from a thousand different viewpoints to discover in it unexpected loveliness. Or it is as if we had heard only one phrase of a symphony, and then heard the phrase again within the whole composition, to have it enlarge and flower in its embodiment and full relationship. Or it is as if we had heard someone described many times and had tried to imagine what he looked like, and then suddenly met him face to face. Our conviction then is that this is what this thing really is. We have a full sense of reality, of being.

To me there is nothing so inexplicable, so disturbing, so mysterious, so religious as this sheer and complete sensuality. It is as if one had been closed inside a dark, stifling room, and suddenly a great wind had torn away the roof and walls to let in a deluge of light and air. What is the cause? Sometimes we can trace it: unexpected good news, sheer good health and vigor, a sudden shock or crisis, a drink, fasting, falling in love, death, danger, anger—and just as often some inexplicable stirring or stimulation. The experience is not always a source of happiness. Often it brings pain, loss, homesickness, grief. But always we feel that we have been torn apart, invaded, deepened.

There are other experiences which have a similar effect, but are characterized by complexity rather than simplicity and identity. These are more likely to arise out of revery and meditation, at the end of long struggles, long periods of stress and pain. Sometimes they come after periods of study and reading, or after we have been rapt for a long time in painting, poetry, and music.

At such times we become aware of an answer to deep and pervading anxieties and wonderments within us. Many things that seemed unrelated and chaotic fall together into patterns of meaning and rightness. Somehow, we do not know by what way, a resolution has come to us. Most often we cannot put it into words. It is perhaps a feeling of emotional rightness more than logical rightness. It is as if, up from that abyss of feelings and sentiency, of raw openness to the world, out of the dark and secret wells of our aloneness and privacy, a knowledge has gathered and broken. It includes too many things, it surrounds too many places for us to define its boundaries. It adds a new facet to every experience that follows it. It surrounds every other person with an incredible tenderness and concern. Somehow every memory, every nerve, every emotion, every cell, is merged into a fullness of selfhood and fellowship. The agony and ecstasy of this awareness cannot be maintained for long. Its intensity exhausts us. If it continues for too long we feel that we are in danger of slipping into the chasm of insanity. But for a time we are able to burn and glow with a new radiance of being. The embers of such hours never quite die away completely.

But do we need to look outside of ourselves and the world about us for an accounting of such states of being? I cannot see why. We live year after year, accumulating within our persons great stores of memories, multitudes of associations and interrelationships of experience. We read many books, know many people, contemplate myriads of ideas. We struggle, yearn, dream, grieve, love, weep, laugh, observe, taste, practice, create—and for months we may not be concerned to ask for meanings or wisdom. But within us, in endless churning and interchange, this amazing confluence of living works upon itself. Below the threshold of consciousness the hidden armies, the underground movements, plot and wrestle. And then there arises a consensus of feeling and evaluation, a single light and heat from the conflagration of a thousand days.

Some people are able to express these perceptions in music and poetry, and we read in them the sister and brother awarenesses that also lie inexpressible within ourselves. Sometimes we can communicate this breaking forth of the mysteries in companionship, when long knowledge, wordless communication of eye and hand tell the unspeakable. There are within us ever new dimensions of knowledge and greatness seeking to be born.

There comes a time when we have become so full of the sun and stars, so burdened with the wastes and infinities of the universe, when our own earth and our own lives have become so intimately woven into the whole, that we seem able to feel and to know the entire firmament whispering within us, every atom of our flesh speaking to every other atom in the world. There comes a time when we are so used by other men, so privy to their sorrows and satisfactions in our years of companionship, that we know within us the meaning of the mass and misery of the whole race. This is mysticism, a mysticism of man in nature.

It comes from the rest of nature around us, converging and

coalescing within that whirlpool of nature which is a human body and person. The universe gathers within a man, speaks and wonders and ponders within him, and then declares to itself the revelation of its own being. The wisdom glows therein, shedding its light on other lives, kindling other fuel with its flame, until the body cools and is received back unto its kindred dust. But as the one spot of turbulence that is a man subsides and disperses, others gather and grow, wherein will be carried to new blossoming that which is the selfhood of nature and man.

⚜ VII ⚜

MYSTICISM AND ETHICS

J. HUTTON HYND

> Mysticism is not a particular religion but a powerful current appearing within all historical religions. Its documents come in vast numbers from Orient and Occident, from times old and new.
>
> KARL WOLFF [1]

THERE ARE VARIETIES of mysticism. The common and characteristic feature of each is the attempt on the part of men and women to "go beyond" the physical and visible "appearances" of our earthly and everyday existence, and so to "solve the mystery" of life. Our awareness of the world by means of the senses is said to be an awareness of *appearances*. Behind the appearance lies a reality. Behind the great illusion lies the ultimate truth. A vision of this ultimate truth will invest human life with ultimate meaning. So say the men and women who practice mysticism. They are the mystics.

Men and women have tried to break through "the veil of sense." They have tried the method of intelligence—hoping, by hard thinking, to catch a glimpse of the Great Reality, the Ultimate Fact. Within the provinces of science and philosophy and logic, by means of investigation and speculation and ratiocination, they have engaged in the quest for certainty. What result has come from their efforts? A little knowledge has been gleaned; but the mystery seems to deepen with every increase of knowledge! J. B. S. Haldane observes: "The advance of scientific knowledge does not seem to make the universe or our life in it less mysterious. It appears to me to be little better than unthinking credulity to

[1] From an address by Karl Wollf as reported in *The Monthly Record* of the South Place Ethical Society, Conway Hall, London.

believe that the mystery has become less deep through scientific advance."

The method of intelligence seeming to have yielded so little, the method of mysticism has been tried. Mysticism places an emphasis upon revelation, or the direct flash of insight which strikes the "inner vision"—perhaps when the eyes are closed against the "mere appearance" of things. (It is said that the word "mysticism" is related to a root which suggests the closing of the eyes.) The great mystery in which reality is veiled, say the mystics, will not yield its secret to the hard human effort of science or philosophy or logic; it will yield finally only as proud and puny man ceases from his mental strife, and learns to wait for the revelation of ultimate reality or ultimate truth. "Be *still*, and *know*," say the mystics to the carnal and restless seekers after knowledge and truth.

It should be pointed out that some believe that there is no opposition between the method of intelligence and the method of mysticism—since the flash of insight may come during a period of quiescent waiting which may follow a period of active thinking; but the distinction to be made between the two methods, as between ratiocination and revelation, may be kept in mind.

The mystics who place most of the emphasis upon revelation profess to know the mystical practices which promise to yield the revelation. There is the practice of emptiness, as when one empties oneself of all awareness of the world and of the earthly self. It is an emptiness which is akin to nothingness. The varieties of mysticism may be known by the varieties of method by which such nothingness and such emptiness may be achieved, as a preliminary to revelation.

The mystics who claim to have received a revelation of reality and truth are wont to say that the revelation cannot be communicated to others by the ordinary means. The others, who would "know the truth," must follow the practice of this or that particular mystic. Particular mystics have frequently organized particular groups of disciples around their own particular methods, thus forming congregations which have become "mystery cults" in which all who practice the prescribed methods are initiated, and are thus permitted to "know the mystery"—to know the truth or particular aspects of the truth, according to the ruling mystic, or according to the congregation.

It may be said, however, that mysticism is not a particular religion; it is a powerful current, flowing in many channels, appearing within all historical religions, as of Orient and Occident, as of old and of new.

It may be profitable to consider four specific kinds of mysticism—a consideration which may lead us to an ethical mysticism.

(1) There is a nontheological and nonethical mysticism. In this form the idea of a god does not appear, and the idea of morality is not prominent. What is sought is just the plain revelation of reality—as of the great impersonal It or That (of neuter gender), the Great Impersonal All. No one can know this *It*, it is said, by ordinary seeing or knowing, but by certain disciplines *It* may be known—as by revelation. The revelation is not an explanation of reality; it is, rather, an experience of reality. The revelation is a feeling of sheer bliss, sheer joy, sheer satisfaction—as when the spirit of the initiate becomes absorbed in the great *It* of the universe. The joy is enjoyed for its own sake—and the experience is enough. It is nontheological and nonethical. The experience lies beyond theological and moral quibbling, say the mystics of this persuasion.

There is a nature mysticism, professed and practiced by certain "nature poets" and some naturalists; but it does not seem to be much more than a sentimental rapture, an emotional ecstasy, arising from an intensive contemplation of nature's "beauty," "benevolence," and "providence." In general, this mystical experience appears to be harmless enough in its theological and ethical neutrality, but there is the danger that it may be too inclined to find its favorite ravishments in the contemplation of the "good" side of nature with blinkers on against a view of the "other" side. Should such mystics turn to the serious consideration of theological and ethical problems they are likely to be sentimental and superficial in their judgments concerning "good" and "evil."

There is a form of nature mysticism which tries to achieve a complete identification with "the invisible and eternal Life of the

One and the All"—believed to be "behind" the illusory appearances of "the natural world" as we *see* it. The mystics who tell us that they have achieved this total absorption "behind the veil" are inclined to say that the experience has taken them "beyond good and evil," beyond all the man-made distinctions and discriminations concerning This and That and right and wrong. When they have "returned to normal" they have appeared among their fellows as having had a revelation of the "truth" that "nothing really matters" apart from this mystical experience of oneness with the life force; they have preached indifferentism and fatalism. They have claimed to have been exalted "above" the petty and pedestrian concerns of mankind with its ambitions and obligations. This ethically indifferent and "spiritually superior" attitude, however, has placed such mystics under condemnation by ordinary men and women who have tried to order their lives in accordance with moral principles in relation to the general good of mankind.

There is the more dangerous nature mysticism which claims to find its deepest and most thrilling experience in the individual's identification with the One and the All as a vaguely impersonal life force, and in terms of its manifestations in sex activity, violence, cunning, cruelty, and so much else of a "vicious" sort. Do we not see on every hand, in nature, an active "malevolence" without discrimination? Then let us have mystic communion with this other side of nature's nature, say certain mystics. This class of mystic surrenders to "nature at its worst," as *we* say. Questions of theology and morality do not enter into this experience. Is it a form of "profane mysticism"? The disapproval and condemnation which this form of mysticism evokes in mankind may be expressed in saying that it asks men and women to be more natural than it is natural for them to be!

There is a very ancient yet very modern claim that a mystical experience is to be found in the use of certain drugs. The experience is *natural* enough, and it is nontheological and nonethical. It is an experience of escape, of withdrawal, and then of return— an experience, it would seem, to be induced and enjoyed for its own sake, or perhaps for the sake of certain beneficial effects upon mind and body. Does this experience suggest a new medical mysticism in which personal problems find their solution in prescribed pills?! In his recent book (1957), *Imagination and Thinking,* Dr. Peter McKellar treats this subject objectively and wisely in the chapter on "The Supernatural and Human Thinking," and with special reference in the section on "Mystical Thinking"; the author warns the reader against the supernatural explanations and interpretations of the many kinds of natural mysticism. The subtitle of the book is *A Psychological Analysis.*[2]

(2) There is a theological form of mysticism. The idea of a god plays a prominent part. The god may be a particular kind of God (as in theism), or he (or she) may be the Great God, the Great "I Am" of the universe (as in pantheism). The personal pronoun is introduced. *It* is now "He" (or "She"). The idea of a god as a person comes into mysticism as a result of a long social and cultural elaboration. The mystic is a creature of his environment. The ideas of the mystic are reflections of the ideas which characterize his culture. Accordingly, within a culture which has elaborated the notion of a god as being a person, the mystic is likely to claim that his revelation is a revelation of the God, or from the God. The mystic may claim that he has "seen God face to face," or that he has "heard the voice of God"—and thus that he has had communion with his God, or the God of his people. Such communion is "bliss beyond compare," the mystic says. The "dark night" of the soul's nothingness and emptiness is illumined as by a great light. The mystic is brought "out of darkness into this most marvelous light." It is an illumination which brings a spiritual satisfaction that is deeper than any other satisfaction known to men.

It should be noted that this satisfaction is an end in itself. It is to "know God" and thus to "know the Truth"—and that is enough. It is the meeting of lovers on the highest plane of pure being. The language of earthly and even of sensual love is perhaps the only language which offers as much as a hint of such an experience to the ordinary mortal. As the presence of the beloved and the consummation of love seem to the human lover to

[2] Peter McKellar, *Imagination and Thinking* (London, 1957).

be the only earthly experience worth living for, so the consummation of the mystic vision in the presence of God and in direct communion with God, is enough for the mystic. Now he knows that God *is*, and that God loves him, and that he loves God. This rapture is an end in itself, and gives meaning to the mystic's life. This rapture of love has no particular meaning beyond itself—either in moral or social terms. In this it is akin to the first form of mysticism considered; it is the idea of the personal God that is added in the second form. The experience, for its own sake, is more personal.

It should be added that this experience of communion with God has been carried farther by some mystics—even to the stage of union with God. "Man is truly God and God truly man . . . If I were not, God were not," says Eckhart, the Christian mystic. The Muslim mystic cries, "Call me not infidel, O my soul, if I say that thou thyself art He." This union with God may have no particular significance beyond itself. It is a purely theological form of mysticism. God is all and in all; and what is more to be desired than this?—asks the god-intoxicated mystic.

(3) We may consider now the theological and ethical type of mysticism. To theological ideas, ethical ideas are added. The God is now more than just a person to be loved and enjoyed for his own sake alone, as by communion and union. The God assumes a moral character. He may be the God of goodness and of grace— the supreme moral value of all moral values. Communion or union with the God may have its effect upon the moral character of the mystic, since the mystic now knows "God's holy will" or is now "a partaker of the divine nature."

The blending of theological with ethical ideas represents an evolution within the social life of mankind. Since ideas of gods are the creations of men, the gods are likely to improve as men improve. As mankind makes progress in its morals it tends to apply its moral standards to its gods. The moral standards of a culture do not come from the gods; the standards emerge within the culture and are then projected upon the gods—as though to receive the sanction of the gods. The gods are now judged by moral standards, and are made to uphold moral standards; and now men refuse to love or worship the gods who may seem to fall short of the accepted moral standards of the people—as the gods so often do when they remain for long periods of time untouched by the moral sense of the community. Thus are the moralized gods created by the conscience of the community.

The development of the conscience of a community is a fascinating subject to pursue, but here the merest report of the pursuit must be given. A community becomes aware of certain forms of behavior that are considered harmful to the group as a whole. The intelligence is operative in this judgment of certain actions. The intelligence takes note of the consequences of such behavior —stealing, killing, bearing false witness, and so on. Such behavior is declared to be bad. But to such a declaration something more is added. The declaration that an act is bad is not enough; and so it is added that such behavior must not be permitted, or ought not to be permitted. There is here an awareness of an obligation; it is the feeling that the bad deed should not be done. To the judgment of the intelligence regarding the badness of an action is added the judgment of the moral sense regarding the wrongness of the action. These judgments may be mistaken—but they are made, and by means of them the conscience of a community is made. This conscience is a composite of intelligence and the moral sense; it is not an infallible guide, but it is a guide—all the better as it becomes more enlightened. And it should be said, of course, that the conscience of a community becomes more enlightened with reference to deeds which should be done as well as with reference to those which should not be done.

The conscience of a community may be projected upon the gods of the community; but let the opinion be expressed here that the conscience of the community, in the first instance, is an affair of the community.

As the gods are creatures of community, so are the mystics. The mystic is likely to take it for granted that the God of the community exists, and that his God has a conscience. The mystic claims to have had a direct communion with his God; but let it be noted that the mystic has come forth from this communion or union as having had more than a mere sense of the rapturous love of God as an experience for its own sake. The mystic has had converse with an ethical God—a God who has concern for the conduct of the people and for the conditions under which the people live, a God who says "thou shalt" and "thou shalt not." The voice of the God and the voice of the conscience are now as one voice. The mystic, as poet, exclaims:

> As feel the flowers the sun in heaven,
> Yet sun and sunlight never see,
> So feel I thee, O God, my God!
> Thy dateless noontide hid from me.
>
> In low estate, I, as the flower,
> Have nerves to feel, not eyes to see;
> The subtlest in the conscience is
> Thyself and that which toucheth Thee.[3]

Thus, a theological mysticism may add morality to its content and become an ethical mysticism; the theological mystic may become an ethical mystic. And let it be said here that the mystic in himself is very often a person of great moral sensibility, even to the extent of going beyond the moral judgments of his own or any other community, and coming forth to make pronouncements regarding morals which may mark an advance in the ethical knowledge of the people, thus hinting the "ever-increasing knowledge, love, and practice of the right." The mystic may be mistaken, but, on the other hand, he may not be mistaken! The great fault of the theological mystic lies in this: that he is likely to claim for his moral pronouncements a "divine sanction" which they do not in reality possess.

It is well to remember here that there is a theological mysticism which claims "divine sanction" for forms of behavior that are judged by some to be immoral in the extreme. For example, it would seem, in so far as we are able to comprehend the system, that over against the devotees of the Hindu God "Vishnu"—a God of Grace who would find incarnation in his devotees—there are the devotees of the Hindu God "Shiva" who seeks human incarnation in terms of sensual orgies and all manner of "disgrace-

[3] Joseph Cook, "The Physical Tangibleness of the Moral Law," *Boston Monday Lectures* (Boston, 1879), pp. 81, 82.

ful practices," his devotees claiming the while to have divine sanction for a "morality" which many judge to be the basest sort of "immorality." It is only fair to say that Hinduism is not alone in this matter of "theological sanction" and the confusion in judgment which may follow concerning morality and immorality.

We have excellent examples of an ethical mysticism as part of a theological mysticism in the Hebrew Prophets—the best of them! Feeling very deeply the seeming low state of morality among the people following a prevalent indifference to the laws of the tribal God, the Prophets came to denounce this dangerous indifference and to call the people back to the moral standards of the Law, or to go beyond the mere letter of the Law to the essential spirit of the Law, which held within it a remarkable spirit of compassion and consideration. There was indeed an ethical emphasis in the words of the Prophets.

The theological thinking of the Hebrews brought an ethical content to religious thought in general; and it is a content which finds a particular expression in the Christian religion. As the more prophetic notion of the Hebrew Messiah assumed the apocalyptic form of "Christ, the Son of God," this Christ, as a living Spirit, assumed the form and the nature of God in the thoughts of many among the Hebrews. This Christ was believed to be the spiritual summation of the ethical concern and compassion and consideration which had found expression in the ancient Law of the Hebrews, and consequently was believed to be a revelation of the nature of Jehovah, the God of the Hebrew people. To make the long story short, a Hebrew sect arose, a sect of mystics, who made the claim that they had had communion with this Christ, yea, union with him, his Spirit absorbing their spirit, thus causing these mystics to become the living and physical representatives of this Christ among men. They proclaimed themselves to be the very "body of Christ"; he walked where they walked, he talked when they talked. This is the mysticism of St. Paul and others. "I live, yet not I, but Christ liveth within me." They formed a nucleus of Christian mystics, following a mysticism at once theological and ethical.

The Christian cult promised to initiate men and women into

the "mysteries of godliness," which were mysteries of god-like-ness; the initiates, by certain rites, were to be "made partakers of the divine nature," were to become "new creatures in Christ," and were to show forth the compassion and consideration of God in Christ in their "daily walk and conversation." The Christian mystics—and all members of the Christian sect professed to be mystics—in their physical and spiritual union with God through Christ, found at once the meaning and the purpose and the impetus of existence, for themselves and for all mankind. The Christian mystics became missionaries, their message being theological and ethical. This theological and ethical mysticism has become a part of our own Western culture.

It should be noted here with emphasis that Christian mysticism has its antinomian and nonmoral aspect—its fundamental aspect, as a matter of fact. The Christian system may be ethical, in the sense that it affects behavior, but, strictly speaking, it cannot be said to be moral. The Christian mystic claims to have mystical experience in terms of "being reconciled to God" and therefore being a "child of God" by mystical identification with the "obedient son" of God; but the Christian mystic does not become a moral person as a result of this, for he is now "above" the moral law under which he has failed so miserably to gain any favor with God. The moral law was simply a schoolmaster whose task was to bring to Christ the sinner who was trying to live a good life "under the law." The law was not "given" that it might be "kept," but that it should be broken so that men might be brought to God "in fear" and discover Him as a God of grace ready to be reconciled to men. By the moral law shall no man or woman be reconciled to God. It is in the sinner's personal and mystical identification with the Christ as the "Son of God" that the Christian becomes "reconciled to God," is made a "child of God," and is made to be "a partaker of the divine nature." "The love of God" is "shed abroad" in the Christian mystic's heart "by the Holy Ghost," and this affects his behavior; but it is not moral behavior. Acting in terms of "divine love," his behavior may seem to be ethically fantastic and foolish in the eyes of men; but this foolishness is said to be "the wisdom of God." This behavior is not "of man"—and the less it appears as "of man" the more it therefore is "of God" (so the dangerous argument runs). This Christian behavior has no real relation to rational and sensible moral behavior, humanly understood; it is different, perhaps actually and really foolish and fantastic, but as such it is dramatic and living evidence of the grace and wisdom of God by means of which this sinner has become reconciled to God and has become a child of God. This reconciliation is all. Christian behavior as such is not moral behavior; it is merely a form of behavior which affords evidence to the believer and to his fellows that he has been "reconciled to God in Christ." Fundamentally, the Christian system is not a moral system; but it may be said that its mysticism has taken a moral turn in certain sects and individuals.

This theological and ethical mysticism of the Christian religion took an interesting turn in the life and thought of Dr. Albert Schweitzer, a theologian who had given special consideration to the mysticism of St. Paul. By family tradition Schweitzer belonged to the sect of Christian mysticism; but his thought and experience led him to a certain interpretation of Christian mysticism which placed more and more emphasis upon the ethical content and less and less upon the theological—the theological content tending to remain as a symbolic and poetic expression of the ethical. Schweitzer came to consider Christ a concept rather than a person; Christ assumed the form of a symbol which suggested a certain quality of spirit, as of compassion and self-denying service. It is a quality of spirit that is to be found in human history and within many religious and social traditions (within the Buddhist tradition, particularly)—a manifestation of the spirit of man on the more ethical side of his nature. Christianity had given to this spirit a definite emphasis. Schweitzer wished to surrender his own spirit to this "Holy Spirit"; he wished to identify himself with "the spirit of Jesus" as the spirit of compassion and consideration. In this identification, Schweitzer is an ethical mystic of a high order, and his mysticism has made its great manifestation in his life as a medical missionary among the needy tribes of Africa.

It should be said that Schweitzer gave emphasis to hard and sincere thinking; and that his clear and cogent thinking had convinced him of the reasonableness of compassion as an ethical force in the affairs of mankind. But his reasoning brought him to reverence, and here we may see the mystic in him. He had a deep feeling of reverence for the spirit of compassion, and he surrendered himself to this feeling as to his thinking. He wished to have communion with it, yea, union with it—and so to become the embodiment of it. From reasoning he went on to reverence—from reverence to devotion. Thus we may see in him a modern example of mysticism—partly theological, but mainly ethical.

(4) There is an ethical mysticism which moves away from theology. The nature of the ethical life may be understood and may be made significant quite apart from the ideas of the gods which men have cherished. Such ideas have a pedigree. Men have looked at the pedigree and have rejected the ideas—not in terms of mere atheistic denial, it should be said. The ideas are rejected because they are neither good enough nor great enough. The ideas have come under man's intellectual and moral judgment; and while they have been found unworthy, they have been found to be unnecessary also. The word "God" explains nothing. To attach the word to ethical values and principles adds nothing and illuminates nothing. On the acceptance of this opinion, an ethical mysticism may be practiced.

In setting morality within its own place, quite apart from theology, we may see that the emphasis is laid upon "the human end of the problem of existence." This humanistic emphasis, which had found articulation in earlier traditions, came to prominence again in the European Renaissance. Indeed, the meaning of the Renaissance is to be found in this resurgence of the humanistic spirit—a spirit which inspired men to the right use of their reasoning powers in their wish to know the nature of the world, and in their attempts to use the resources of the world for the achievement of a good life on earth. Since ethics plays an important part in such an achievement, the study of human conduct assumed prominence and in due course led to the discovery that morality as a discipline may take its independent place among the disciplines, and may gain in stature by being divorced from theology.

We may note, then, that the humanistic interpretation of the moral life has an association with rationalism. Rationalism insists upon the use of reason in all matters pertaining to morality. It insists upon intellectual discipline and intellectual honesty. It advocates the open-eyed approach to life. If a man wishes to live according to moral principles, then let him no longer bow his head and close his eyes before mere arbitrary and authoritarian pronouncements concerning morality; let him lift up his head, open his eyes, and stand upon his feet, and let him comprehend the nature of the moral life with all its principles and obligations; and in keeping with his comprehension, let him freely and gladly place himself under the discipline of an ethical way of life.

Thus reasoning and honest thinking may bring a man to the recognition of the mystery of moral obligation. Reduce morality to mathematical precision, if you will; the mystery of morality (like the mystery of mathematics) remains. Mysteriously, as Kant suggests, the laws and principles of the moral life, being related to the Good Life which men wish to achieve, become the laws of Duty, having their own "categorical imperative" and making their demands upon our devotion. Reasoning may bring a man to the place where he feels the sublimity of the moral life, and where reverence for the moral law is awakened in him. The feeling may be nonrational, but it is not irrational. Rationalism, to be consistent, must give a place to reverence as an emotion, and in due course must give a place to the devotion which intelligence and reverence may inspire.

Accordingly, as by reasoning men may see the true nature of the moral life, apart from theological associations, and may admit the validity and sublimity of moral values and principles, so by reasoning men may be brought to the place of dedication where they may wish—with open eyes—to submit to the disciplines of the moral life, gladly as well as dutifully. In this rational and emotional submission to the demands of the moral life we may come very near to the practice of mysticism—an ethical mysticism in which men may be said to love the good and to wish to be united in mind and spirit with the great tradition of the good life, and so to be the living embodiments of its grace and its creative power in the affairs of mankind. Moral ideas are "poor ghosts" until they find embodiment "in the flesh," and until they become active in all the relations of daily life.

This ethical mysticism may be said to have kinship with the mysticism of Albert Schweitzer; but in this fourth form of mysticism there are no theological implications, even of the symbolic and poetic sort. It may be granted that such symbolism and poetry may have a legitimate place within a rational scheme (as all symbolism and poetry may have a place); but it is well to take special note here of an ethical life and an ethical mysticism which have no affiliations whatsoever with theological speculations and supernatural explanations.

An ethical mysticism such as this, being divorced from theology, may yet be religious in spirit, since there are to be found within it the elements of reverence for the principles and ideals of a good life, and of devotion to the fulfillment of ethical principles in personal and social life. The view is taken here that the gods of the more primitive and popular religions were created and called in to subserve the human search for values believed to be good. Alfred North Whitehead, in *Religion in the Making*, says: "The peculiar character of religious truth is that it explicitly deals with values"—knowledge of values, reverence for values, devotion to values; and he proceeds to say significantly:

> Religious truth must be developed from knowledge acquired when our ordinary senses and intellectual operations are at their highest pitch of discipline. To move one step from this position toward the dark recesses of abnormal psychology is to surrender finally any hope of a solid foundation for religious doctrine.[4]

Accordingly, although there are mysticisms and religions which have ignored the moral obligation of intellectual honesty and which have plunged downward to the dark depths of "abnormal

[4] Alfred North Whitehead, *Religion in the Making* (New York, 1926), pp. 123-24.

psychology," we may have an ethical mysticism and an ethical religion that are sane and sensible, and eminently practical. Felix Adler in his *Religion of Duty* and *An Ethical Philosophy of Life,* and John Dewey in *A Common Faith,* approach the precincts of an ethical and truly religious mysticism, and even enter the precincts and bid others enter, open-eyed and erect, with all the ordinary "senses and intellectual operations at their highest pitch of discipline."

It should be noted here that Felix Adler in New York, and Stanton Coit in London, England, as ethical mystics, proceeded to organize Ethical Culture Societies as religious fellowships within which, by means of public services, preaching and teaching, open discussion and other methods, men and women and children might be initiated, so to speak, into the mysteries and glories and obligations and satisfactions of the ethical life as an expression of the religious life on its higher reaches—without theological pronouncements or commitments. The Ethical Culture Society in New York is "dedicated to the ever-increasing knowledge, love, and practice of the right"; and in the services of the Ethical Church in London the Introit was heard:

> Let Knowledge grow from more to more,
> But more of Reverence in us dwell,
> That mind and soul according well
> May make one music as before—but vaster.

In a pamphlet entitled *The Ethical Movement as Seen from Within,* Dr. Horace J. Bridges says,

> A sentence of St. Isidore reads: "Wherefore dost thou wonder, O Man, at the height of the stars or the depth of the sea? Enter into thine own soul and wonder there." We have sought to do this, not only in the mystical spirit, but above all in the ethical, and, I may add, in the rational spirit. We have entered into the soul of man not only to wonder but to inquire, and if possible to explain.

It were as though the founders, leaders, and members of such Societies had said with George Croly:

> I ask no dreams, no prophet-ecstasies;
> No sudden rending of the veil of clay;

No angel-visitant, no opening skies;—
But take the dimness of my soul away.[5]

It might be said, then, that the safest and sanest mysticism for
man to practice—since mystery confronts him on every side—is
an ethical mysticism which stands apart from dogmatic theology.
It is a mysticism which respects the method of intelligence and
which asks men and women to think—to think clearly, regarding
the best possibilities of the Good which appear within the natural order, "on this side of the veil," so to speak, and within
human history; and having so given thought, men and women
are invited to submit themselves, in reverence, dedication, and
devotion, to the "vital principle of betterment"—that thus they
may become religious devotees of "an ever-increasing knowledge,
love, and practice of the right," in domestic relations, in civic relations, in labor and business and professional relations, and in international relations, and that thus they may know some of the
deepest emotional satisfactions within their reach, and may create
the ethical and spiritual—and the material and social—conditions
under which mankind may achieve and fulfill the good life in all
its variety and fullness.

There is here a rational and yet a mystical identification of the
self with that "continuous human community" which lives always
in the present; it is a mystical identification with the human effort to achieve a good life—not as a "far-off divine event to which
the whole creation moves," not as looking forward to human perfection, and not as ignoring the problem of natural and human
"evil," but as a partial and yet satisfying achievement within each
generation, according to its capacity and opportunity; since the
meaning of life, it is suggested, is not to be found at the end of the
human story but within the human story at every moment of consciousness. An ethical mysticism of this kind suggests that life at
every moment is "saturated with values," and that we must learn
to open our eyes, and to enter into the mystery of goodness, a
mystery which makes high demands upon intelligence, emotion,

[5] George Croly, Hymn No. 48, *Hymns of the Spirit* (Boston, 1937).

and will. "Identify yourself with mankind," said Felix Adler who, in fact, has been spoken of as "mystic and man of action":

> Identify yourself with mankind. Think of yourself as a disciple of Prometheus, and as part of man's life through the ages. Carry the past into the present. Study history, not with a view of knowing all the facts, for that is impossible, but so as to come into contact with those great moments in which humanity put forward a living effort, and so that you too may receive the contagion of the effort.[6]

[6] Felix Adler, *Our Part in This World* (New York, 1946), p. 1.

☙ VIII ❧

MYSTICISM AND THE LIMITS
OF COMMUNICATION

JOHN A. IRVING

D URING the nineteenth century the idealism of Hegel dominated philosophical thought in Western culture. Idealism
had a breadth, an authority, and a speculative insight into
ultimate reality unrivaled by any subsequent system. Its expo-
nents were the critics not only of science and theology but of all
other special approaches to reality. Idealists performed their distinctive philosophical function from the standpoint and in the
name of a reality transcending all human and temporal limitations. But for all its speculative grandeur and quasi-religious
inspiration, idealism failed to mold the temper of twentieth-century Western culture.

At the beginning of the twentieth century the long dominance
of the Hegelian philosophy in Europe and America was already
drawing to a close. During the period from 1900 to 1925 the most
conspicuous new movements in philosophy were the phenomenology of Edmund Husserl in Europe; the pragmatism of Charles
Peirce, William James, and John Dewey in the United States; and
the new realism of Bertrand Russell, G. E. Moore, and Samuel
Alexander in England. The latter tendency was also represented
in the United States, in a somewhat different form, by such men
as E. B. Holt, E. G. Spaulding, W. P. Montague, and R. B. Perry.

Of these new movements, the greatest impact on the public
mind was made by the American pragmatists. They attempted to
exhibit philosophy as a creative and liberating agency in ongoing human activity. Emphasizing the nexus of theory and practice, they studied the psychological and sociological functions of
philosophical ideas. Confronted with the rawness of a pioneer
civilization, they proclaimed their faith in the capacity of man's

99

intelligence to solve all issues raised in the flow of time. In the instrumentalist version of Dewey, pragmatism fashioned North American educational philosophy for succeeding generations. But it also raised to the level of self-conscious knowledge in Western culture the broadest implications of science, democracy, evolution, and progress.

Today, phenomenology, pragmatism, and realism, while they still have articulate champions, are receding into the past. Having driven out German idealism, they have been challenged during the last thirty years by three new approaches. The latest movements, in the order of their appearance, are: (1) logical analysis (also called in its various manifestations, logical positivism, logical empiricism, therapeutic positivism, and linguistic analysis); (2) existentialism; and (3) the meeting of East and West tendency (not yet academically christened) under the brilliant and energetic leadership of F. S. C. Northrop. In addition to these three movements, two great systems of philosophy developed in the past—Thomism and Dialectical Materialism—enjoy today the official favor of the Roman Catholic Church and the Communist Party respectively.

Existentialism,[1] the second of the most recent movements, has been discussed in the present volume by Professor Newton P. Stallknecht. Certain aspects of the third movement have likewise been considered by Professor N. A. Nikam in his chapter on some ontological and ethical aspects of mysticism in Indian thought.

The third tendency in contemporary thought may be considered as a phase of the ecumenical movement in its largest aspects. For Northrop, there are two valid approaches to reality—the conceptual approach of the philosophical and scientific traditions of Western culture and the mystical approach of the religious traditions of Oriental cultures like Hinduism and Buddhism. The limitations of Western culture may be overcome by the acceptance of the Asian way to Nirvana.[2]

[2] For an exposition of Northrop's philosophy see his *Meeting of East and*
[1] For an exposition of the present writer's attitude to existentialism see his *Science and Values* (Toronto, 1952), Chapter IV, "Thoughts on Existentialism."
West (New York, 1952).

Significantly enough, logical analysis, the most dynamic and influential of the three contemporary movements in Western philosophy, also takes us to mysticism. In the present chapter it is proposed to examine certain phases of the philosophy of logical analysis, with the object of showing the significance of this approach for mysticism.

In its immediate origin, logical analysis arose out of the realistic reaction to British idealism under the leadership of Bertrand Russell and G. E. Moore. But the sources of its widespread influence today are to be found in many other aspects of modern philosophy, science, and culture. Philosophically, logical analysis may be traced on the one hand to Hume's empiricism and on the other hand to developments in mathematical logic arising out of the work of George Boole, Gottlieb Frege, G. Peano, Bertrand Russell and A. N. Whitehead. Scientifically, its development was influenced by the methodological writings of Karl Pearson, Henri Poincaré and Ernst Mach. All of these tendencies converged in the luminous mind of Ludwig Wittgenstein, who published in 1921 his *Tractatus Logico-Philosophicus*.[3]

Culturally, the philosophy of logical analysis mirrors the intellectual climate of today. The intellectual qualities popular in our culture are detachment, subtlety, professionalism. As Mr. John Holloway has brilliantly commented, one can trace clearly in the new philosophy that has developed from Wittgenstein's work

> the modern intellectuals' distrust of pious, fine-sounding, vague generalities, the scientists' admiration for minute and dispassionate analysis, a complexity and subtlety like that typical of all the contemporary arts, and in its later stages an emphasis on organic and functional enquiries as in ecology or modern anthropology or economics. One should remember this continuity with our whole contemporary culture, if only in justice to the subject; for philosophy

[3] It is now fashionable to say that Wittgenstein effected two, quite different, transformations in modern philosophy. Be that as it may, the present chapter is concerned entirely with the doctrines set forth in the *Tractatus*. It must be insisted, however, that Wittgenstein never forgot the two propositions of the *Tractatus* that are essential for our present interpretation: (1) *Philosophy is not a theory but an activity;* (2) *Whereof one cannot speak, thereof one must be silent.*

is far too often accused nowadays of shirking its traditional responsibilities to man and society, and retiring into a linguistic hairsplitting isolation.[4]

The work of Wittgenstein, the central figure in the philosophy of logical analysis, was made possible by Frege's discovery that natural numbers are not found in experience like the color "blue" but are concepts by postulation, and by Russell's discovery that the linguistic form of a proposition is not always identical with its logical form. These discoveries caused a technical convulsion in philosophy. Russell's more restricted proposals for the resolution of the philosophical difficulties that arose as a result of these developments were generalized by Wittgenstein into a comprehensive program for the future of philosophy. This was a fateful step in the history of philosophy, a step that could have been taken only by a man of genius. Wittgenstein was a genius.

In a paper on "The Future of Philosophy" presented at the Seventh International Congress of Philosophy at Oxford on September 5, 1930, Moritz Schlick declared that the truth about the real function of philosophy was first seen with absolute clearness by Ludwig Wittgenstein. Schlick then recommended to the philosophical world Wittgenstein's view that philosophy is neither a set of doctrines nor a theory, but an activity. "The object of philosophy," Wittgenstein had announced in the *Tractatus,* "is the logical clarification of thoughts," and he had then continued:

> Philosophy is not a theory but an activity.
> A philosophical work consists essentially of elucidations.
> The result of philosophy is not a number of "philosophical propositions," but to make propositions clear.
> Philosophy should make clear and delimit sharply the thoughts which otherwise are, as it were, opaque and blurred.[5]

Such is the basic creed of the philosophers of logical analysis.

With the above brief account of the background of the philosophy of logical analysis in mind, I shall now offer my interpreta-

[4] John Holloway, "The New Philosophy of Language in England," *The Hudson Review,* IV (1951), 448.

[5] Ludwig Wittgenstein, *Tractatus Logico-Philosophicus* (London, 1922), prop. 4.112, p. 77.

tions of: (1) the assumptions and method of logical analysis; (2) the philosophical implications of this method; and (3) how this method, in the version of logical analysis (not necessarily my version) presented in Ludwig Wittgenstein's *Tractatus Logico-Philosophicus,* leads to mysticism.

Underlying the philosophy of logical analysis, as I interpret it, is an assumption that the development of pure logic and of the psychology of communication has brought to light the cardinal philosophical problem of our time, that of the meaning of meaning. The view of the problem implied in pure logic is that there are no synthetic a priori propositions. The propositions of logic and of mathematics are a priori, but only because they are analytic; the propositions of science are synthetic, but only because they are a posteriori. The denial of synthetic a priori propositions profoundly changes the status of philosophy.

The view of the problem implied by the psychology of communication is that only the formal structure of experience, and never its content, can be communicated. When we deny that the immediately given in experience can be communicated we are making a profound change in the status of the theory of knowledge, and emphasizing anew the importance of the logic of relations.

Philosophy, for those who work with the twentieth-century temper, is essentially the elucidation and clarification of the meanings of propositions, words, and concepts. A proposition is a symbolic representation or expression of a fact or a situation, and a fact or a situation can always be expressed in the form that *so and so is the case.* The meaning of a proposition is its verifiability, and it cannot have meaning unless there is a possibility of indicating how it may be verified or refuted. We verify a proposition by exhibiting the structure of the situation to which it refers, and the process is complete when we have shown that the situation is made up of specific constituents, logically related in a specific way. In this connection it is most important to notice that we are constantly dealing with the objects of our thought, as well as with the thinking. We must examine the situation to which a proposition refers, not merely the proposition itself.

We can claim to know a proposition only when we can state exactly in what sense it is meaningful, and such a statement would imply that we are able to exhibit the structure of the situation to which the proposition refers. We must always seek to discover, therefore, in the search for the meaning of a proposition, the data which verify the proposition, if they are the case. When we have discovered these data we must be able to express their relationship to each other by a proposition whose logical structure mirrors the structure of the situation to which it refers. This proposition points to the situation and exhibits its structure.

The philosophical activity of elucidating the meaning of a proposition reveals the structure of the situation which we know to be the case, and leads to a criticism and revision of our fundamental beliefs about the situation and its structure. If we cannot discover the situation that would verify a proposition, then that proposition is not one which we can truly claim to know. The philosophical elucidation of propositions is thus something more than mere examination of language, or than the laying down of rules for the combinations of symbols. Philosophy enables us both to say clearly what we really know when we declare a proposition is true, and to distinguish those propositions which it is possible to verify, and therefore to know, from those which cannot be verified and therefore cannot be known.

Research in the psychology of communication has shown that most of our words and concepts have varying degrees of subjective and objective reference. On the subject of the nature of words and concepts there is a certain accord in the findings of sociologists, psychologists, and logicians, which indicates a constant drive toward extreme nominalism. Words are remotely conditioned substitutes for conditioned stimuli to action; since they have been produced by environmental pressure it follows that their meaning can extend only as far as their reference to atomic facts. The nature of language cannot be other than the nature of such stimuli.

Every concept has both an objective and a subjective reference. The meaning of a complex word or concept is given by explicit definition; that of a simple word or name by pointing to what it stands for in experience. The meaning of a term or concept is best discovered by observing what we *do* with it, not by what we *say* about it. A concept refers to nothing more than a class of properties; the reference of the concept is synonymous with the corresponding class of properties; i.e., a scientific concept is a label for a class of properties that can be investigated scientifically. What is the meaning of the concept of x? An intelligible answer can be given only when we translate the question into the form: what conditions determine x and its manifestations in (1) observable behavior, (2) the logical structure of a situation y? The only intelligible meaning of the concept x is to denote collectively the properties of the class y.

Logical analysts admit that people do use language in other senses than we have described above, e.g., in poetry. But language used in this way cannot communicate that which is meaningful as knowledge. We must distinguish between propositions which we can verify and therefore know, and emotive utterances which we cannot verify and therefore cannot know. The former propositions give us objective knowledge (verifiable belief); whereas the latter merely induce us to take up a subjective emotional attitude toward something in our experience, the experience of others, or our external environment.

These distinctions raise the profound problem of the logic of our language. The origin of language is not the philosopher's concern; the uses to which language has been put in the past and is put in the present will occupy our attention exclusively here. Many logical analysts consider that there are two uses of language —the scientific and the emotive.

We use language scientifically when we use it in propositions which (1) are constructed in accordance with the rules of logical syntax; (2) have an unambiguous reference, true or false (the "being-the-case" or the "not-being-the case"). We use language emotively when we use it for the sake of the effects in emotion and attitude produced by the reference it occasions. Speculative philosophy and all the sciences, except mathematics and those parts of physics and chemistry that can be expressed in mathematical or symbolic form, are still more or less in a state of confusion owing to an elementary misunderstanding of these two uses of language.

When we use language scientifically, the reference is to *our public world* of socially communicable meanings, in which the concepts have a specific value (they tell us how to proceed); in which every proposition has a meaning that can be given in terms of a public exhibition of the structure of the situation to which it refers; in which thought is guided at every stage by the brute resistance of the material. Emotive language, by contrast, refers to *my private world* of immediately perceived contents, of passionate desires, of eager wishes. My thought, meeting with no brute resistance from its material, conjures up endless vistas of references to which I *may* give emotive assent.

The business of philosophy, as many logical analysts understand it, is to separate clearly the public and the private worlds, and then to elucidate the meanings of the public world, which are otherwise opaque and blurred.

Logical analysis substitutes elucidated for unelucidated knowledge. I now ask the profound question: *Is this the only kind of knowledge that philosophy can give us?* Traditionally philosophers have maintained that there are two sources of human knowledge—the a priori and the a posteriori. According to his dominant temper each philosopher has attributed greater or less constructive weight to these two factors. So that in a very real sense the history of philosophy has been, as William James saw clearly, a certain clash of human temperaments.

The a posteriori temper proceeds cautiously toward generalizations based on analogies from immediate experience; the a priori temper, confidently relying on the synthetic activity of the logical reason, proceeds by way of inevitable deductions from self-evident logical principles. Now it seems quite clear today that philosophical knowledge is not *in itself* derived from immediate experience. It seems equally clear that philosophical knowledge is knowledge of self-evident logical principles.

The nature of philosophical knowledge turns therefore on the nature of self-evident logical principles. What is the nature of the a priori? Are there any synthetic a priori propositions? Kant answered this question affirmatively by taking to witness the propositions of logic, mathematics, and natural science. But twentieth-century investigations into the nature of these propositions challenge Kant's answer in all three fields.

More especially, research concerning the nature of necessary inference or formal implication seems to have demonstrated that all self-evident propositions have a very definite kind of logical structure. As Blumberg and Feigl have so clearly put it, "Logic in the wide sense is shown to be a system of conventions which determine the syntactical order required if we are to have a consistent language." Wittgenstein has emphasized that the propositions of logic are tautologies. Whenever we can truly say that p implies q, where p and q are propositions, the truth conditions of q are included in the truth conditions of p. Since a proposition is the expression of its truth conditions, it follows that all such propositions are tautologies:

> The propositions of logic are tautologies.
> The propositions of logic therefore say nothing. (They are the analytical propositions.) . . . .
> The fact that the propositions of logic are tautologies *shows* the formal-logical-properties of language, of the world.[6]

Therefore, the logical reason does not synthesize, and necessary inference is transformed into a type of analysis which selects one element from a complex and ignores the other elements. Hence the discovery of logically necessary truths is also a result of the elucidation of our knowledge, and cannot be interpreted as the discovery of new facts.

Besides the knowledge gained through immediate experience and the knowledge of necessary truths, there is the knowledge that we get from science. This appears to be the knowledge of probabilities, based on data we get from immediate experience, according to the logical principles of probability in so far as they are agreed upon. This scientific knowledge represents an attempt to achieve a unified conception of nature; and regard for the principles of probability makes it clear that the so-called "scientific method" is the best way of making such an attempt.

[6] *Ibid.*, props. 6.1, 6.11, 6.12, pp. 155-57.

What sort of knowledge does there remain for philosophy to give us? The knowledge of first principles falls under the knowledge of self-evident logical principles, and has been shown to depend on the elucidation of unelucidated knowledge. There is Cosmology, which is an attempt to achieve a unified conception of nature; but so is science. The principles of probability make it clear that the difference between the two is that the scientific method is the better one and even that can only give us more or less probable conclusions.

Another possible activity for philosophy is the so-called speculative philosophy, which consists in formulating a system which will, provisionally at least, organize all other forms of knowledge. But the substitution of elucidated for unelucidated knowledge itself organizes all forms of knowledge by making clear exactly what our knowledge involves. Is there any other method of organizing all forms of knowledge? For many logical analysts there is not. The field of scientific knowledge nowadays is so vast that no one person can possibly assimilate it. If we limit ourselves to some particular field there seem to be only two alternatives: either to proceed according to scientific methods, or else to elucidate unelucidated knowledge already gathered in that field.

There is thus no point in speculating on the implications of various scientific discoveries. If the speculators are philosophers, the value of their speculations is usually vitiated by their imperfect understanding of science; and if they are scientists, their speculations are usually worthless owing to their philosophical incapacity. Speculation on the implications of scientific discoveries is a fascinating way to spend one's time; but such speculations give us knowledge of such small probability as scarcely to be worthy of the name. Our knowledge of the facts in question can either be added to by further scientific analysis, or else elucidated by the methods of logical analysis.

The philosophy of logical analysis implies, of course, that metaphysical propositions are, strictly speaking, meaningless, since a proposition has meaning only when we know under what conditions it is true or false. If the meaning of a proposition is its verification, it cannot have meaning unless there is a possibility of indicating how it may be verified or refuted. The propositions of metaphysics, whether of the dialectical or intuitive variety, are admittedly incapable of empirical verification, and hence they cannot give us *meaningful* knowledge.

Belief in the efficacy of dialectical metaphysics is based, as Blumberg and Feigl have so clearly realized, upon—

> failure to see the tautological or analytical nature of all necessary inference or formal implication. Since deductibility is tautological, the conclusion can not contain logically any more than is asserted in the premises of the argument, in this case empirical sequences. Nor is dialectical demonstration in the sense of a merely probable inference to entities beyond experience permissible. Probable inference is but another name for argument by analogy or by induction. Such argumentation is valid only in empirical questions, where the possibility of subsequent empirical verification of the conclusion is present.[7]

Belief in the efficacy of intuitive metaphysics is based upon the confusion of knowledge with immediate noncognitive experience, as well as upon the ignoring of all logical and empirical factors. Intuitive metaphysics is thus the vain attempt to describe the content of experience, to express the inexpressible, to utter the unutterable—in logical language. Intuitionist metaphysicians have built for themselves a kingdom of metaphor. They have made words their viziers; logically the core of their intuition is a fluent blur. These considerations suggest that the limits of human communication and of philosophical discourse are rather rigidly confined. *"The limits of my language,"* says Wittgenstein, "mean the limits of my world."

During the last twenty-five years the denigration of metaphysics has been an important part of the program of logical analysts. Many of them have taken more or less seriously Wittgenstein's injunction concerning the right method of philosophy, an injunction given toward the close of the *Tractatus:*

> The right method of philosophy would be this. To say nothing except what can be said, i.e. the propositions of natural science, i.e. something that has nothing to do with philosophy: and then al-

[7] A. E. Blumberg and H. Feigl, "Logical Positivism," *The Journal of Philosophy,* XXVIII (1931), 294.

ways, when someone else wished to say something metaphysical, to demonstrate to him that he had given no meaning to certain signs in his propositions. This method would be unsatisfying to the other —he would not have the feeling that we were teaching him philosophy—but it would be the only strictly correct method.[8]

With a fine consistency Wittgenstein then admits that the propositions in terms of which he has led us to understand his theory are themselves propositions which that theory itself condemns as meaningless:

> My propositions are elucidatory in this way: he who understands me finally recognizes them as senseless, when he has climbed out through them, on them, over them. (He must so to speak throw away the ladder, after he has climbed up on it.)
>
> He must surmount these propositions; then he sees the world rightly.[9]

At the very moment the reader is prepared to challenge the status of the propositions on which the philosophy of logical analysis rests, he finds that Wittgenstein has unexpectedly done the trick for him. The propositions that need to be expressed in constructing the philosophy of logical analysts are propositions which that philosophy itself condemns as meaningless.

Once Wittgenstein has challenged the meaningfulness of the propositions he has used in constructing the philosophy of logical analysis, he is only one step removed from mysticism. He does not hesitate to take the final step. "Whereof one cannot speak," the *Tractatus* concludes, "thereof one must be silent." [10] The only consistent philosopher is the silent mystic, for the inexpressible contains the whole of logic and philosophy. Thus the long and arduous quest for certainty ends, once again, in mysticism.

But, in leading us to mysticism, the philosophy of logical analysis illuminates as never before the real nature of the inexpressible. Philosophy takes us to the inexpressible by clearly displaying the expressible:

> Everything that can be thought at all can be thought clearly. Everything that can be said can be said clearly.

[8] Wittgenstein, *op. cit.*, prop. 6.53, pp. 187-89.

[9] *Ibid.*, prop. 6.54, p. 189.

[10] *Ibid.*, prop. 7, p. 189.

Propositions can represent the whole reality, but they cannot represent what they have in common with reality in order to be able to represent it—the logical form.

To be able to represent the logical form, we should have to be able to put ourselves with the propositions outside logic, that is outside the world.

Propositions cannot represent the logical form: this mirrors itself in the propositions.

That which mirrors itself in language, language cannot represent.

That which expresses *itself* in language, *we* cannot express by language.

The propositions *show* the logical form of reality.

They exhibit it. . . .

What *can* be shown *cannot* be said.[11]

Wittgenstein's attitude toward the mystical is the natural outcome of his doctrine in pure logic. But, in spite of their logical impeccability, his conclusions concerning the limits of meaningful communication leave one with a certain sense of intellectual discomfort, as even Bertrand Russell acknowledges. The mind may be left unsatisfied, but I believe that Wittgenstein has offered a brilliant solution of the paradox that has baffled Western mystics in all ages—the paradox of the expression of the inexpressible. He solves this paradox by leading us, through the philosophy of logical analysis, to realize that the mystical can be shown, although it cannot be said. "There is indeed the inexpressible. This *shows* itself; it is the mystical."

Although Wittgenstein distinguishes sharply between the expressible and the inexpressible, he himself manages to make, toward the close of the *Tractatus,* a number of beautiful comments about the ultimate nature of the world and life:

Not *how* the world is, is the mystical, but *that* it is.

The contemplation of the world *sub specie aeterni* is its contemplation as a limited whole.

The feeling of the world as a limited whole is the mystical feeling.

For an answer which cannot be expressed the question too cannot be expressed.

The riddle does not exist.

[11] *Ibid.,* props. 4.116, 4.12, 4.121, 4.1212, pp. 77-79.

If a question can be put at all, then it *can* also be answered.

Skepticism is *not* irrefutable, but palpably senseless, if it would doubt where a question cannot be asked.

For doubt can only exist where there is a question; a question only where there is an answer, and this only where something *can* be *said*.

We feel that even if *all possible* scientific questions be answered, the problems of life have still not been touched at all. Of course there is then no question left, and just this is the answer.

The solution of the problem of life is seen in the vanishing of this problem.

(Is not this the reason why men to whom after long doubting the sense of life became clear, could not then say wherein this sense consisted?)

There is indeed the inexpressible. This *shows* itself; it is the mystical.[12]

These piercing statements themselves belong, as Wittgenstein admits, to the realm of the mystical—of what can be shown but not said. Nevertheless, they illuminate profoundly the nature of the mysticism that flows from the philosophy of logical analysis. They indicate, also, that Wittgenstein himself must have had mystical experiences in their purest form.

As far as I am aware, Wittgenstein's mysticism has never been formally designated or classified. In view of the importance of logical syntax in its development, this type of mysticism may appropriately be called syntactical mysticism.

Syntactical mysticism has more in common with orthodox Western mysticism than with Oriental mysticism. Theistic Western mysticism is related to the mathematical *Logos,* while Oriental mysticism arises from the radical empiricism of sensed immediacy. Imbedded as it is in pure logic, syntactical mysticism represents an important development in, and clarification of, Western mysticism, rather than a contribution to Oriental mysticism. In spite of the divergent foundations of syntactical mysticism and Oriental mysticism, it is noteworthy that to many Asian mystics the philosophy of logical analysis is the most congenial of the contemporary schools of Western thought.

12 *Ibid.,* props. 6.44, 6.45, 6.5, 6.51, 6.52, 6.521, 6.522, p. 187.

SOME ASPECTS OF ONTOLOGICAL AND ETHICAL MYSTICISM IN INDIAN THOUGHT

N. A. NIKAM

Communication and Silence

IT IS SAID: "For the East the intuitive 'higher' knowledge is not capable of verbal expression and communication, at least to those who have not attained it." [1] But it is necessary to distinguish between a situation (a) in which there is no expression or communication because two persons do not speak the same language, and (b) where, as in Logic, a thing is indefinable because it is *understood*. The case of higher intuitive knowledge is like (b). "The indefinable does not therefore mean that which is presented as having no understood meaning, but whose meaning is so directly and universally understood, that it would be mere intellectual dishonesty to ask for further definition." [2] The *Katha Upaniṣad* says: "Not by speech, not by mind, not by sight can He be comprehended. How can He be comprehended otherwise than by saying, 'He is.' " [3] The "comprehension" is an awakening which cannot be conveyed or communicated. [4] Communication may be possible by other means than verbal expression: by silence,

[1] Charles A. Moore (ed.), *Essays in East-West Philosophy* (University of Hawaii, 1951), p. 429.

[2] W. E. Johnson, *Logic* (Cambridge, 1921), I, 106.

[3] R. E. Hume (ed.), *The Thirteen Principal Upanishads* (London, 1931), *Katha Upanishad,* 6.12.

[4] "The Zen masters . . . have faced a very difficult task in trying to convey what they have within themselves. Strictly speaking, however, there is no conveying at all. It is the awakening of the same experience in others by means of words, gestures, and anything the master finds suitable at the moment. There are no prescribed methods; there is no methodology already set down in formulas." Daisetz Teitaro Suzuki, "Zen: A Reply to Hu Shih," *Philosophy East and West,* III, 1 (April, 1953), 36.

and by the living together of master and pupil. In the *Praśna Upaniṣad* six pupils intent on the search of Brahma approached the teacher Pipplāda and requested him to expound the doctrine. The teacher said to them: "Dwell with me (*samvatsyatha*) a year (*samvatsara*) with austerity (*tapas*), chastity (*brahmacharyā*), and faith (*śraddhā*). Then ask what questions you will." "Living together" is a process of communication. The Upaniṣads say: *upaśānto 'yam ātma:* "The self is silence." I cite the following passage from the conversations of a contemporary Indian mystic:

Disciple. Is a vow of silence useful?

Master. The inner silence is self-surrender. And that is living without the sense of ego.

D. Is solitude necessary for a Sannyasin?

M. Solitude is in the mind of man. One might be in the thick of the world and yet maintain perfect serenity of mind; such a person is always in solitude. Another may stay in the forest, but still be unable to control his mind. He cannot be said to be in solitude. Solitude is an attitude of the mind; a man attached to the things of life cannot get solitude, wherever he may be. A detached man is always in solitude.

D. What is *Mouna* (silence)?

M. That state which transcends speech and thought is *Mouna;* it is meditation without mental activity. Subjugation of the mind is meditation; deep meditation is eternal speech. Silence is everspeaking; it is the perennial flow of "language." It is interrupted by speaking; for words obstruct this mute "language." Lectures may entertain individuals for hours without improving them. Silence, on the other hand, is permanent and benefits the whole of humanity. . . . By Silence Eloquence is meant. Oral lectures are not so eloquent as Silence. Silence is unceasing Eloquence. . . . It is the best Language. There is a state when words cease and Silence prevails.

D. How then can we communicate our thoughts to one another?

M. That becomes necessary if the sense of duality exists. . .

D. Why does not Bhagavān go about and preach the Truth to the people at large?

M. How do you know I am not doing it? Does preaching consist in mounting a platform and haranguing the people around? Preaching is simple communication of Knowledge; it can really be done in Silence only. What do you think of a man who listens to a sermon for an hour and goes away without having been impressed by it so as to change his life? Compare him with another, who sits in a holy Presence and goes away after some time with his outlook on life totally changed. Which is better, to preach loudly without effect or to sit silently sending out Inner Force? Again, how does speech arise? There is abstract Knowledge, whence arises the ego, which in turn gives rise to thought, and thought to the spoken word. So the word is the great grandson of the original source. If the word can produce effect, judge for yourself, how much more powerful must be the Preaching through Silence! [5]

Subject and Object

The distinction between knowledge by acquaintance and knowledge by description is now well known. The two are different in some important respects but are concerned with the external world. In the epistemology of mysticism, there is a sense of

[5] Śri Ramanāśraman, *Maharshi's Gospel* (Tiruvannamalai, Madras Province, India, 1949), Books I and II, pp. 15-16. The following passages may be cited from the conversations of Śri Ramana Maharshi published recently:

"Disciple. *Has God a form?*
Master. Who says so?
D. Well, if God has no form is it proper to worship idols?
M. Leave God alone because He is unknown. What about you? Have you a form?
D. Yes, I am this and so and so.
M. So then, you are a man with limbs, about three and a half cubits high, with beard, etc. Is it so?
D. Certainly.
M. Then do you find yourself so in deep sleep?
D. After waking I perceive that I was asleep. Therefore by inference I remained thus in deep sleep also.
M. If you are the body why do they bury the corpse after death? The body must refuse to be buried.
D. No, I am the subtle *jīva* within the gross body.
M. So you see that you are really formless; but you are at present identifying yourself with the body. So long as you are formful why should you not worship the formless God as being formful.

The questioner was baffled and perplexed." (Pp. 162-63.)

"D. *What is Renunciation?*
M. Giving up of the ego.

acquaintance which must be reached by negating this sense of acquaintance. As the *Kena Upaniṣad* puts it: *nedam yadidam upāsate:* "not that which you *think,*" i.e., not that which you think *about* (as an object). The two senses of acquaintance correspond to two senses of *That:* (a) That which is seen by the eye; (b) That by which the eye sees. *Yac cakṣuṣā na paśyati yēna cakṣūṁṣi paśyati tad eva brahma tvam viddhi:*

> That which is not seen by the eye but by which the eyes are seen (see), know that as Brahma.[6]

Reality—*Atman* or *Brahman*—is the "That," in the second sense:

> whereby what has not been heard of becomes heard of; what has not been thought of becomes thought of; what has not been understood, becomes understood.[7]

Mysticism is neither dogmatism nor agnosticism but true gnosticism; it requires two propositions to state its theory of knowledge: (a) we are in contact with the Real; (b) the Real transcends our knowledge. This double position is expressed in the dialogue

---

D. Is it not giving up possessions?

M. The possessor too.

D. The world will change if people will give up their possessions for the benefit of others.

M. First give yourself up and then think of the rest." (P. 206.)

The Paradox of Self-realization: "The 'I' casts off the illusion of 'I' and yet remains as 'I.' Such is the paradox of Self-Realization. The realized do not see any contradiction in it. Take the case of *bhakti* (devotion). I approach God and pray to be absorbed in Him. I then surrender myself in faith and by concentration. What remains afterward? In place of the original 'I,' perfect self-surrender leaves a residuum of God in which the 'I' is lost. This is the highest form of devotion (*parābhakti*), *Prapatti,* surrender or the height of *Vairāgya.*" (P. 44.) T. N. Venkataraman, *Talks with Ramana Maharshi* (Tiruvannamalai, India, 1955), Vol. I.

[6] *Kena Upaniṣad,* I, 7. In the New York meeting of the Metaphysical Society (March, 1953), a speaker defined reality as "the terminal object" of knowledge. Will it be enough if reality is defined as the "terminal" of knowledge? How do we know that reality is the terminal *object?* I put this question to the speaker.

[7] Hume, *op. cit., Chāndogya Upaniṣad,* 6.1.3.

between the teacher and the pupil in the *Kena Upaniṣad*. The teacher says to the pupil:

If you think "I know well" only very slightly, now do you know a form of Brahma!

The pupil replies:

I think not "I know well"; yet I know not "I know not." [8]

Reality in the Upaniṣads

The Upaniṣads are an expression of man's primal awareness of the mystery of Being. The *Śvetāśvatara Upaniṣad* asks:

What is the cause? Brahma? Whence are we born?
Whereby do we live? And on what are we established?
Overruled by whom, in pains and pleasures,
Do we live our various conditions, O ye theologians? [9]

The unity of being is the ultimate affirmation of the Upaniṣads. The unity is reached by affirming the identity of the ground of individual psychical existence and of the world. There are two questions asked: (a) What is the real Agent in the individual? and (b) What is behind the experienced world of objects? The *Kena Upaniṣad* asks concerning individual existence:

By whom willed and directed does the mind light on its objects? By whom commanded does life the first, move? At whose will do (people) utter this speech? And what god is it that prompts the eye and the ear? [10]

The psychology of this passage presupposes that the physical, the vital, and the mental functions are not self-explanatory but are grounded upon something which manifests itself through them; or, perhaps, does not fully manifest itself. Says Emerson:

The soul in man is not an organ, but animates and exercises all the organs; it is not a function, like the power of memory, of calcula-

[8] *Ibid., Kena Upaniṣad*, 9-10.
[9] *Ibid., Śvetāśvatara Upaniṣad*, I, 1.
[10] S. Radhakrishnan (ed.), *The Principal Upaniṣads* (London, 1953), *Kena Upaniṣad*, I, 1.

tion, of comparison, but uses these as hands and feet; is not a faculty but a light . . . an immensity not possessed and that cannot be possessed.[11]

The *Muṇḍaka Upaniṣad* asks concerning phenomenal existence: "By knowing what, Sir, is all this known?" *Kasmin nu bhagavo vijñāte sarvam idam vijñātam bhavati.* In the *Nature of Existence,* McTaggart thinks that there is a sufficient description of substance which implies—without including sufficient descriptions of the infinite sets of parts of substance such that we need not know the last of the infinite series of sets of parts (which would be a contradiction)—that we can know the nature of substance. The *Muṇḍaka Upaniṣad* asks for a knowledge of the infinite variety of the world of objects without knowing *all* of them. It is not a demand for coherence nor for a major premise from which knowledge of other things in the universe could be deduced. The philosophy of mysticism is not a search either for a self-evident principle or a principle of noncontradiction. The *Iśa Upaniṣad* ascribes contradictory predicates to Brahman:

> It moves and It moves not; It is far and It is near; It is within all this and It is also outside all this.[12]

Reality is not the subject of contradictory predicates, nor of that which is self-consistent and merely free from contradiction. The conception of Reality in the Upaniṣads exceeds the notions of coherence and comprehensiveness. The upaniṣadic quest is for the discovery, in one's own self, of the inner soul of all things. It is not noncontradiction but identity or nonduality, rather than coherence and formal consistency or system, which is the criterion of reality and truth in the philosophy of the Upaniṣads:

> These rivers, my dear, flow, the eastern toward the east, the western toward the west. They go just from the ocean to the ocean. They become the ocean itself. As there they know not "I am this one," "I am that one"—even so, indeed, my dear, all creatures here, though

[11] Brooks Atkinson (ed.), *The Complete Essays and Other Writings of Ralph Waldo Emerson* (New York, 1940), p. 263.
[12] S. Radhakrishnan, *op. cit., Iśa Upaniṣad,* 5.

they have come forth from Being, know not "We have come forth from Being." Whatever they are in this world, whether tiger, or lion, or wolf, or boar, or worm, or fly, or gnat, or mosquito, that they become.

That which is the finest essence—this whole world has that as its soul. That is Reality. That is *Ātman*. That art thou: *"tat tvam asi."* [13]

R. E. Hume states:

> If there is any one intellectual tenet which, explicitly or implicitly, is held by the people of India, furnishing a fundamental presupposition of all their thinking, it is this doctrine of universal immanence, of an intelligent monism.[14]

What are the ethical implications of this fundamental presupposition of Indian thought to life and to civilization? Albert Schweitzer says in his autobiography that he was in search of an ethical principle which could connect philosophy with civilization, where the will-to-progress ceases to be merely an external pursuit of knowledge and power, and affirms a truly ethical attitude to life and civilization. Schweitzer discovered this principle in "Reverence for Life":

> The iron door had yielded: the path in the thicket had become visible. Now I had found my way to the idea in which affirmation of the world and ethics are contained side by side! Now I knew that the ethical acceptance of the world and of life, together with the ideals of civilization contained in this concept, has a foundation in thought.[15]

The universal immanence and monism of the Upaniṣads is the foundation in thought for the ethics of reverence for life. Reverence for life is a necessary corollary of the upaniṣadic monism. There is no "superior speaker" other than he who affirms the

[13] Hume, *op. cit., Chāndogya Upaniṣad*, 6.10.1-3: *tat tvam asi,* "That Thou Art," is a proposition yet to be verified in the living experience of the pupil. The verification is the affirmation: "I am Brahman."

[14] Hume, *The Thirteen Principal Upanishads,* 2nd ed. (London, 1931), p. 2.

[15] Albert Schweitzer, *Out of My Life and Thought,* C. T. Campion, tr., (New York, 1949), pp. 156-57.

ethics of the universality of life and reverence for life. Says the *Muṇḍaka Upaniṣad:*

> Truly it is Life *(Prana)* that shines forth in all things! Understanding this one becomes a knower. There is no superior speaker.[16]

The affirmation of life, the will to live through the will to promote life everywhere, not negating or doing "injury" *(ahimsā)* to life, this is the essence of the ethics of the Upaniṣads. And Schweitzer points out:

> The great fault of all ethics hitherto has been that they believed themselves to have to deal only with the relations of man to man. In reality, however, the question is what is his attitude to the world and all life that comes within his reach. A man is ethical only when life, as such, is sacred to him, that of plants and animals as that of his fellow men.[17]

The ethics of the Upaniṣads is not the ethics of the relation of man to man only, but a feeling of responsibility for all that lives, a fellowship with all that lives. The ethics of the relation of man to man is only a particular relation of the universal ethics of *ahimsā* (noninjury) or reverence for all life. This may be described as the ethical mysticism, the unity of all life, of the Upaniṣads.

The doctrine of universal immanence is a doctrine of spiritual monism or nondualism and the universal *Ātman* is identical with the essential nature of our psychical existence; therefore, there is the Vedāntic affirmation: *Jivo Brahmaiva:* "The individual soul is Brahman and is not other than It." The individual soul is identical with Brahman, the indestructible ground of the universe, the *akṣara;* the soul "is never born nor does it die at any time"; *najāyate mrīyate vā Kadācin.*

> Brahma, indeed, is this immortal. Brahma before,
>   Brahma behind, to right and to left:
> Stretched forth below and above,
>   Brahma, indeed, is this whole world, this widest extent.[18]

---

[16] Hume, *op. cit., Muṇḍaka Upaniṣad,* 3.1.4.
[17] Schweitzer, *op. cit.,* pp. 158-59.
[18] Hume, *op. cit., Muṇḍaka Upaniṣad,* 2.2.11.

The presence of reality in all appearances and the deathlessness of
Ātman are coexistent doctrines. There is no "ceasing to be" because there is no "coming to be" of *Ātman*. The fear of "ceasing
to be" is the cause of man's anguish. Myth and religion have their
origin in fear but their aim is to show that fear is a myth;
abhayam hi vai Brahma: "Brahman, indeed, is Fearlessness." The
desire for immortality is not for the mere continuance of this life.
Ati dīrge jīvitum ko rametā? (Kaṭha): "Who wants to live too
long?" is not a cry for the extinction of the will to live, but a
quest for an existence which is not minus value. The mystery of
Being is not probed and the anxiety of life is not overcome if
man's desire is to escape fear and sorrow, for there is a gap between the absence of fear and sorrow and the creative inspiration
of the delight of existence. Says the *Brihad-Āraṇyaka Upaniṣad:*

> In the beginning this world was Soul (Ātman) alone in the form of a
> Person. Looking around, he saw nothing else than himself. He said
> first: "I am" . . .He was afraid. Therefore one who is alone is afraid.
> This one then thought to himself: "Since there is nothing else than
> myself, of what am I afraid?" . . . Verily, he had no delight. There-
> fore one alone has no delight.[19]

Fear and sorrow have a common origin in man's loneliness of
spirit, in his failure to see the unity of all Being, in his failure to
actively realize fellowship with all Being; *tatra ko moha kaḥ
sokah ekatvam anupaśyathaḥ:* "Where is delusion or sorrow for
him who sees oneness?" [20]

Ananda or the Delight of Existence

Mysticism is an active affirmation of life and not the negation
of world and life. This is so in the Upaniṣads. There is the invocation in the *Kena Upaniṣad:*

> May my limbs grow vigorous, my speech, breath, eye, ear as also my
> strength and all my senses. All is the *Brahman* of the Upaniṣads.
> May I never discard *Brahman*. May the *Brahman* never discard

[19] *Ibid., Brihad-ārnyaka Upaniṣad,* 1.4.1-3.
[20] Radhakrishnan, *op. cit., Isá Upaniṣad,* 7.

me. May there be no discarding. May there be no discarding of me. Let those truths which are (set forth) in the Upaniṣads live in me dedicated to the self. *Aum,* peace, peace, peace.[21]

That there is no "ceasing to be" is not the whole meaning of immortality. The *Gita* says: "Thou shouldst not grieve"; *nānu śocitum arhasi.* Why? Because there is "survival"? The *Gita* does not mean this. If we should not grieve because there is "survival," then the just man and the unjust man are both immortal. "On what principle, then, shall we choose justice rather than injustice?" [22] Mysticism must provide an answer to this question; the mere affirmation of deathlessness of the soul is not a foundation in thought for an active affirmation of life. It is "immortality in work or action," *karmasu ca amṛtam,* that is a true affirmation of immortality.

Mysticism is the awareness of the reality of the invisible. It is the perception of the unseen; it is the affirmation of the unseen in the visible. It is the affirmation of life amidst universal death. It is the active affirmation of the delight of existence in a chaotic and dark world. It is the affirmation of the principle in creation whereby the world has come to be. This principle is *ānanda,* the delight of existence: the creative principle whereby the original solitariness and fear of the Person (*Puruṣa*) behind creation, is overcome by Himself by His act in creating the world. Creation is a sharing of the delight of existence: "The Lord of Creation (*Prajāpati*), verily, was desirous of offspring (*prajā*)." [23] The meaning of human life is discoverable in the principle behind creation: *anandāt eva khalu imāni bhutāni jāyante:* "out of delight, verily, these beings have come into being." As Śri Aurobindo explains:

> Absoluteness of conscious existence is illimitable bliss of conscious existence: the two are only different phrases for the same thing. All illimitableness, all infinity, all absoluteness is pure delight.[24]

[21] *Ibid., Kena Upaniṣad,* Invocation, 1-3.
[22] *The Dialogues of Plato,* B. Jowett, tr., with an introduction by Raphael Demos (New York, 1937), *The Republic* 2.366.
[23] Hume, *op. cit., Praśna Upaniṣad,* 1,4.
[24] Śri Aurobindo, *The Life Divine* (Calcutta, 1949), I, 115.

The Chandogya Upaniṣad says: *na alpe sukham asti bhumiva sukham:* There is no pleasure in the small. Only a Plenum is Pleasure (bhumān).

What is a Plenum?

> Where one sees nothing else, hears nothing else, understands nothing else—that is a Plenum. But where one sees something else—that is the small. Verily, the Plenum is the same as the immortal; but the small is the same as the mortal.
>
> That plenum, Sir—on what is it established?
>
> On its own greatness—unless, indeed, not on greatness at all.[25]

And Tagore goes so far as to say that the criterion of truth is gladness:

> Gladness is the one criterion of truth as we know when we have touched Truth by the music it gives, by the joy of the greeting it sends forth to the truth in us. That is the true foundation of all religions, it is not in dogma.[26]

So the poet sings:

> Joy! Joy! I triumph! Now no more I know
> Myself as simple me. I burn with Love.
> The Center is within me, and its wonder
> Lies as a circle everywhere about me.
> Joy! Joy! No mortal thought can fathom me.
> I am the merchant and pearl at once
> Lo! Time and space lie crouching at my feet. . .
> I plunge into myself and all things know.[27]

The delight of existence (*ānanda*) is not a mere rapture or ecstasy, a transient state, an intellectual perception, but an active life seeking affirmation in action. The delight of existence is mysticism in practice: *ātma-krīḍa ātma-ratiḥ kriyāvān eṣā brahma-vidāṁ variṣṭaḥ:* sporting in the self, delighting in the self, performing works, such a one is the greatest of the knowers of

---

[25] Hume, *op. cit., Chāndogya Upaniṣad*, 7.24.

[26] Rabindranath Tagore, "The Religion of an Artist," J. H. Muirhead and S. Radhakrishnan (eds.), *Contemporary Indian Philosophy*, 2nd ed. (London, 1952), p. 33.

[27] Gurdial Mallik, *Divine Dwellers in the Desert* (Bombay, 1949), p. 11.

Brahman.[28] The mystic affirmation of life and of the delight of existence is a free outpouring of a liberated consciousness. It is incapable of resting even as the living God Himself does not rest. The mystic consciousness frees itself from all attachments, enters into the stillness of the self, and yet breaks forth into activity without compulsion, without seeking for reward, and without the egoism of thinking that it alone can save the world. The mystic consciousness is thus free from Hamlet's cry: "Oh, cursed spite that ever I was born to set it right."

There are at least three senses or ways in which *ānanda* or the delight of existence manifests itself:

(a) The delight of existence (*ānanda*) is a capacity to *receive* things in a spirit of equanimity: *sama dukha sukham:* "an equality in pain and pleasure." This is not "indifference." It is a gladness issuing from the self-discovery that you are free to receive the effects of things upon you in the way *you* choose: "I have reached a stage when even the aches come only as a form of *ānanda*." [29]

(b) The delight of existence is the affirmation of the "I am" in the "Thou art," a conquest of the isolation of the "I am":

> The fact that we exist has its truth in the fact that everything else does exist, and the "I am" in me crosses its finitude whenever it deeply realizes itself in the "Thou art." This crossing of the limit produces joy, the joy we have in beauty, in love, in greatness. Self-forgetting, and in a higher degree self-sacrifice, is our acknowledgment of this our experience of the infinite.[30]

The problem of the delight of existence is how to be, or have "the courage to be," in a chaotic and finite world. Our actions tend to involve us in a vicious regress and they threaten the reality of our freedom. The delight of existence is not a fact unless we can act as free beings in the spirit of creative joy.

(c) The rule of action which reveals the *ānanda* or delight of existence is action in the spirit of *Yajna*, "sacrifice," an act of self-giving: *Yajnarthāt karmano 'nyatra loko'yam karmabandhanaḥ:* "Save work done, as and for sacrifice this world is in bond-

[28] Radhakrishnan, *op. cit., Muṇḍaka Upaniṣad,* III, 1.4.
[29] *Some New Letters of Śri Aurobindo* (Pondicherry, 1949), p. 20.
[30] Tagore, *op. cit.,* p. 36.

age to work." [31] The motive of action as "sacrifice" or self-giving exceeds even the notion of action as duty for the sake of duty; sacrifice means self-giving which is a delight, an affirmation of the delight of being, "an experience of the infinite."

The idea of sacrifice is ancient; it is present in all religions. In primitive religions it is an act of propitiation performed in fear of the supernatural. It is naturalistic, utilitarian, egotistical, and unethical. It is selfish, for it is performed to obtain some private gain here or hereafter. But the idea of sacrifice is much more meaningful than this. Sacrifice is the "myth" behind Creation, *sahayajanāḥ prajāḥ sṛṣṭvā purō'vācā prajāpatiḥ*: "In ancient days the Lord of creatures created men along with (or by an act of) sacrifice." [32] Creation is an act of the self-giving of the "Lord of creatures" (*Prajāpati*). The rule for us as human beings is the performance of all actions for the sake of the Divine.

The ancient idea of sacrifice stands for equality and social solidarity. The social significance of this ancient idea is now revived in our country by the practical mystic, Ācharya Vinoba Bhave, Mahatma Gandhi's disciple, in his social conception of *Bhōōdān-Yajna,* "the offer of land as sacrifice" (and not as mere "charity") as a solution of the land problem in our country—indeed, as a solution of its many economic and social problems. The idea of *Yajna* exceeds the idea of "charity." In an act of charity the recipient is obliged to the giver and there is no true equality between them. In an act which is a *Yajna* the recipient is under no obligation to the giver; what is given belongs to *all* and the act of giving is a reaffirmation of the essential equality of *all* in a social order.[33] He who acts in the spirit of sacrifice is a

[31] *Gītā*, III.9.

[32] *Gītā*, III.10.

[33] The basic idea behind *Bhōōdān-yajna* is *Samya-yoga,* which has ontological and ethicosocial significance. *Samya-yoga* is based on the fundamental idea of *samatva* (equality), the idea that the spirit is immanent equally in all beings, the idea which is the basis of the upaniṣadic monism, the ideal of *Sarvodaya* society, a society which provides for full and free development of *all* (and not merely of the majority, or the greatest happiness of the greatest number). *Samya-yoga* seeks to revolutionize society but thinks it wrong to associate revolution with violence. Revolution can be brought about only

samya-yogi, "the practicer of equality," in a genuine sense and not a *samya-vādi,* the totalitarian and doctrinaire egalitarian who imposes equality on a social order by violence, taking away the essential freedom of the act of self-giving which is the basic truth behind Creation.

Higher Knowledge and Lower Knowledge

Mysticism rests upon the distinction between two kinds of knowledge. The Upaniṣads distinguish between *parā-vidya* or "higher knowledge" and *a-parāvidya* or "lower knowledge." The higher knowledge is the clue to the understanding of the world. "Through the understanding of what, Sir, is all this understood?" It is through the understanding of higher knowledge that "all this," *sarvamidam,* is understood. The higher knowledge is knowledge of the *akṣara,* the Eternal, while the "lower knowledge" is of the various special sciences and arts or empirical studies: pronunciation (*śikṣā*), ritual (*kalpa*), grammar (*vyākaraṇa*), definition (*nirukta*), metrics (*chandas*), and astrology (*jyotiṣa*).[34]

This is an indication of the kind of empirical studies meant by lower knowledge, but not an exhaustive enumeration of them. Plato asks in *The Republic:*

> "What," he said, "is there a knowledge still higher than this—higher than justice and other virtues?" "Yes," he said, "there is. . . . The idea of the Good is the highest knowledge, and that all other things become useful and advantageous only by their use of this." [35]

Plato draws a distinction between the "skilled mathematician" and the "dialectician." The dialectician is one who is able "to give and take a reason"; he reasons "by the light of reason only without the assistance of sense and does not rest until by pure intelligence he attains pure good." "Lower knowledge" gives

through a change of values. *Samya-yoga* brings about this change of values because it takes its stand upon a spiritual view of things. See "Revolution Through *Samya-Yoga*" (Ahamedabad: Navajivan Press), *Harijan,* November 7, 1953.

[34] Hume, *op. cit., Muṇḍaka Upaniṣad,* I.1.5.

[35] *The Republic* 6.504-505.

"skill," proficiency, expertness; it is "useful," i.e., "if pursued with a view to the beautiful and the good . . . but if pursued in any other spirit, useless." [36]

The Upaniṣads rank as "lower knowledge" not only empirical studies but even the formal study of the scriptures, the "traditions" of religion, dogma, ritual, etc. The *Gītā* calls persons who are limited to the study of the mere traditions of religion the "undiscerning," *avipascitah*.[37] They rejoice in the letter of the Veda (or Scripture), *Vedavāda ratāḥ*. They are intent on heaven, *svargaparā*, and they contend that there is nothing other than the dogmas and traditions of religion: *na'nyad asti 'ti vādinaḥ*. The *Muṇḍaka Upaniṣad* speaks of rituals as "unsafe boats" for crossing from mortality to immortality: *adṛḍā yajnarupā*.[38] The *Gītā* uses a telling analogy to illustrate the formal study of Scripture as dogma, compared to the active realization of the Divine in life. It says:

> As is the use of a pond in a place flooded with water everywhere, so is that of all the Vedas for the Brahmin who understands.[39]

So the *Katha Upaniṣad* speaks of the two kinds of knowledge, higher and lower, as "widely opposite and asunder," *Duram ete viparīte viṣūci*.[40] Higher knowledge is *Brahmavidya*, it is the foundation of all knowledge, *sarva vidyā pratiṣṭām*, and is immemorial and more ancient than the traditions of religion. Its origin is in the original myth of the descent of the Divine into the human. It is a knowledge that is "communicated" or "received":

> Brahma arose as the first of the gods—the maker of all, the protector of the world. He told the knowledge of Brahma (*brahma-vidyā*), the foundation of all knowledge, to Atharvān his eldest son.[41]

What Atharvān received was handed down by him to Angir, and so on in the unbroken continuity of the Tradition. The Tradition

---

[36] *Ibid.*
[37] *Gītā,* II, 42-43.
[38] Hume, *op. cit., Muṇḍaka Upaniṣad,* 1.2.7.
[39] *Gītā,* II, 46.
[40] Hume, *op. cit., Katha Upaniṣad,* 2.4.
[41] *Ibid., Muṇḍaka Upaniṣad,* 1.1.2.

of *Brahmavidya* as the foundation of all knowledge is the same Tradition of old, but it is also new: it receives new confirmation in the living experience of generations of teachers and their pupils from age to age. The ultimate authority of *Brahmavidya* is not in mere doctrine or dogma but in the living experience of the "knowers of Brahma," the mystics, the seers, the teachers, prophets, and the God-intoxicated souls.

The audacious freedom of the human spirit in its realization of the divine in life, expressed in the Upaniṣads in the knowledge of the *parāvidya* as knowledge of the Eternal, finds renewed expression in contemporary times in India in the mystical philosophy of Śri Aurobindo. He says in that ancient largeness of spirit of the Upaniṣads:

> For the sadhaka of the integral Yoga it is necessary to remember that no written *shastra*, however great its authority or however large its spirit, can be more than a partial expression of the eternal Knowledge. He will use but never bind himself even by the greatest Scripture.[42]

The Sādhaka of the integral yoga is not the "Sādhaka of a book or of many books; he is a Sādhaka of the Infinite." Yoga is the realization of the Infinite:

> We not only seek the Infinite, but we call upon the Infinite to unfold himself in human life.[43]

Freedom from authority or dogma is another name for the infinite receptivity of the human spirit; and accordingly the active realization of the divine in life requires an infinite receptivity in the human soul:

> An absolute liberty of experience and of the restatement of . . . the knowledge received from the past.[44]

The seeker of eternal knowledge "must live in his own soul," as the Gita states it, and exceed "the [mere] written Truth, *sabdabrahmātivartate*." [45]

[42] Aurobindo, *The Synthesis of Yoga*, 1st ed. (Madras, 1948), p. 4.
[43] *Ibid.*, p. 6.
[44] *Ibid.*, p. 5.
[45] *Ibid.*, p. 4.

Parāvidya and *aparāvidya* are "widely asunder and opposite." It is in this context that the poetical and negative passages of the Upaniṣads occur:

> There the eye goes not; speech goes not, nor the mind. We know not, we understand not, how one would teach it.[46]

> This Soul (Ātman) is not to be obtained by instruction, nor by intellect, nor by much learning.[47]

> That which is invisible, ungraspable, without family, without caste (*a-varṇa*), without sight or hearing is It, without hand or foot, Eternal, all-pervading, omnipresent, exceeding subtile; That is the Imperishable, which the wise perceive as the source of beings.[48]

> The sun shines not there, nor the moon and stars, these lightnings shine not, where then could this fire be? Everything shines only after that shining light. His shining illumines all this world.[49]

The most important characteristic of thought in the Upaniṣads is inclusiveness, which finds expression in alternative standpoints: (a) Brahman is *neti, neti,* "not-this," "not-this"; and (b) "Brahman is, indeed, all this": *sarvam khalu idam Brahma.*[50] Brahman

[46] Hume, *op. cit., Kena Upaniṣad,* 1-3.

[47] *Ibid., Kaṭha Upaniṣad,* 2.23.

[48] *Ibid., Muṇḍaka Upaniṣad,* 1.1.6.

[49] Radhakrishnan, *op. cit., Muṇḍaka Upaniṣad,* II.2.11.

[50] The perspective of the mystic consciousness is an affirmation of comprehension inclusive of all that is: its transcendent inclusiveness and its transcendent greatness in excluding everything is powerfully expressed in two verses of the *Avadhuta-Gita:*

sarvatra sarvadā sarvaṁ ātmānaṁ satataṁ dhruvaṁ
sarvaṁ śūnyam aśūnyaṁ ca tan māṁ viddhi na saṁśayaḥ.

"Everywhere, always, in all, know the Ātman to be the enduring or the abiding. Know me as all, void and the nonvoid. There is no doubt about this."

vedāḥ na lokāḥ na surā na yajnaḥ varṇāśramo naiva kulaṁ na jātiḥ
na dhūma-mārgo na ca dipti-mārgo brahmaika-rūpaṁ paramārtha-tattvam.

"There is neither scripture, nor worlds, nor gods, nor sacrifices, no classes nor stages of life, neither race nor caste, neither the way of smoke nor the path of flame. Ultimate Reality which is *Brahman* is alone manifest. It is the Highest Reality." (His Highness Śri Jaya Chamarajendra Wadiyar Bahadur, *Dattatreya: The Way and the Goal;* Intr. by Radhakrishnan [London, 1957], p. 167.)

is all this because all this *is* Brahman. Both these attitudes are freedom from the notion of "either or." The inclusiveness of this standpoint finds expression negatively in the notion of "neither" and positively in the notion of "both and." Reality is conceived both as personal and impersonal, immanent and transcendent, etc. This is an inclusiveness which appears to be consistent with relativity of standpoint.

Mahatma Gandhi: Truth is God

This characteristic of ancient Indian thought is discoverable in the great contemporary Hindus. Mahatma Gandhi derives his conception of Truth (*satya*) and *Ahimsā* (nonviolence or noninjury) from it. The Upaniṣads affirm an identity: Atman = Brahman; Mahatma Gandhi affirms the identity: Truth = God. His religion is a progress from "God is Truth" to "Truth is God." The following two passages from Mahatma Gandhi's writings are important:

> To me God is Truth and Love; God is ethics and morality; God is fearlessness. God is the source of Light and Life and yet He is above and beyond all these. God is conscience. He is even the atheism of the atheist. For in His boundless love God permits the atheist to live. He is the searcher of hearts. He transcends speech and reason. . . . He is a personal God to those who need His personal presence. He is embodied to those who need His touch. He is the purest essence. He simply is to those who have faith. He is all things to all men. He is in us and yet above and beyond us.
>
> He is the greatest democrat the world knows, for He leaves us "unfettered" to make our own choice between evil and good. He is the greatest tyrant ever known, for He often dashes the cup from our lips and under cover of free will leaves us a margin so wholly inadequate as to provide only mirth for Himself at our expense. Therefore it is that Hinduism calls it all His sport—*Līla,* or calls it all an illusion—*Maya.* We are *not,* He alone Is. And if we will be, we must eternally sing His praise and do His will.[51]

In the following passage, Mahatma Gandhi explains how he made a transition from "God is Truth" to "Truth is God":

[51] M. K. Gandhi, *Hindu Dharma* (Ahmedabad, 1950), p. 61.

You have asked me why I consider that God is Truth. In my early youth I was taught to repeat what in Hindu scriptures are known as one thousand names of God. But these one thousand names of God were by no means exhaustive. We believe—I think it is the truth—that God has as many names as there are creatures and, therefore, we also say that God is nameless; and since God has many forms we also consider Him formless, and since He speaks to us through many tongues we consider Him to be speechless, and so on. And so when I came to study Islam I found that Islam, too, had many names for God. I would say with those who say God is Love, God is Love. But deep down in me I used to say that though God may be Love, God is Truth, above all. *If* it is possible for the human tongue to give the fullest description of God, I have come to the conclusion that for myself, God is Truth. But two years ago I went a step further and said that Truth is God. You will see the fine distinction between the two statements, viz., that God is Truth and Truth is God. And I came to that conclusion after a continuous and relentless search after Truth which began nearly fifty years ago. I then found that the nearest approach to Truth was through love. But I also found that love has many meanings in the English language at least and that human love in the sense of passion could become a degrading thing also. I found too that love in the sense of *ahimsa* had only a limited number of votaries in the world. But I never found a double meaning in connection with Truth and even atheists had not demurred to the necessity or power of truth. But in their passion for discovering truth the atheists have not hesitated to deny the very existence of God—from their own point of view rightly. And it was because of this reasoning that I saw that rather than say that God is Truth I should say that Truth is God.[52]

The Integral Yoga of Śri Aurobindo

Śri Aurobindo's integral Yoga is a philosophy of evolution. It restates the upaniṣadic mysticism in the light of a new experience. Life is the field of integral Yoga: the transformation of human life into life divine and integral Yoga is a new birth. Indeed, "All yoga is a new birth." Integral Yoga is not *one* of the aims in life but the whole aim of life. Integral Yoga is a self-directed evolution.

Integral Yoga is an integrated inner and outer existence. Its philosophy is radically distinct from those types of religions and

[52] *Ibid.,* pp. 66-67.

schools of Yoga which separate the life of the world from inner life. These schools of religion, intimates Śri Aurobindo, appear to think that—

> the powers of this world and their actual activities do not belong to God at all or are for some obscure and puzzling cause, *Māya* or another, a dark contradiction of the divine Truth.[53]

These schools are based on the antinomy of an "either or"; and so there arises in these schools the necessity of an exclusive concentration upon the One and an uncompromising renunciation of the world. But integral Yoga is not for this exclusive concentration and individual salvation; in integral Yoga, says Śri Aurobindo:

> We have set out to conquer all ourselves and the world for God. . . . The Divine that we adore is not only a remote extracosmic Reality, but a half-veiled Manifestation present and near to us here in the universe. Life is the field of a divine manifestation not yet complete: here, in life, on earth, in the body—*ihaíva,* as the Upaniṣads insist,—we have to unveil the Godhead; here we must make its transcendent greatness, light and sweetness real to our consciousness, here possess and, as far as may be, express it. . . . Victorious in the struggle, we can compel Earth herself to be an aid toward our perfection and can enrich our realisation with the booty torn from the powers that oppose us.[54]

Two powers are operative in the process of integral Yoga: a power of Aspiration from below and a power of Descent of the Divine and its Grace from above:

> There are two powers that alone can effect in their conjunction the great and difficult thing which is the aim of our endeavor, a fixed and unfailing aspiration that calls from below and a supreme Grace from above that answers.[55]

Integral Yoga is a process of upward and downward movement: of ascent and descent and the two aspects of one movement or evolution.

[53] Aurobindo, *op. cit.,* p. 26.

[54] *Ibid.,* pp. 27, 28.

[55] Aurobindo, *The Mother* (Pondicherry: Śri Aurobindo Ashram, 1949), p. 1.

This movement or evolution with its two aspects is termed a sacrifice, *yajna:* its meaning and the symbolism are of the greatest significance to integral Yoga. Ascent and descent are both sacrifice; for the Divine existence sacrifices itself in creation: the One existence becomes the Many; "Would that I were Many," as the Upaniṣads say: *prajākāmaḥ prajā patiḥi:* "The Lord was desirous of offspring." The ascent from below which is an aspiration is also a sacrifice: it is a sacrifice of the ego, a self-surrender to the Divine. In a sense, the sacrifice of the ego is going on in nature *unconsciously* through defeat and negation; this is the tragedy in the human drama. In integral Yoga this tragedy is converted into *ānanda* or the delight of existence through a conscious and self-consecrated sacrifice to the Divine and its operations. This act of conscious sacrifice and self-consecration is a proof or recognition that the ego is not alone in the world nor chief in the world. Says Śri Aurobindo:

> The law of sacrifice is the common divine action that was thrown out into the world in its beginning as a symbol of the solidarity of the universe. It is by the attraction of this law that a divinising, a saving power, descends to limit and correct and gradually to eliminate the errors of an egoistic and self-divided creation. This descent, this sacrifice of the *Purusha,* the Divine Soul submitting itself to Force and Matter so that it may inform and illuminate them, is the seed of redemption of this world of Inconscience and Ignorance. . . . The acceptance of the law of sacrifice is a practical recognition by the ego that it is neither alone in the world nor chief in the world. It is its admission that, even in this much-fragmented existence, there is beyond itself and behind that which is not its own egoistic person, something greater and completer; a diviner All which demands from it subordination and service. Indeed, sacrifice is imposed and, where need be, compelled by the universal World Force; it takes it even from those who do not consciously recognize the law,—inevitably, because this is the intrinsic nature of things.[56]

The meaning of sacrifice has been misunderstood in religious tradition; it is understood to mean a mere negative, unenlightened act of torture and self-immolation, a kind of starvation,

[56] Aurobindo, *The Synthesis of Yoga,* p. 67.

as it were. In integral Yoga, however, this is not the case. Sacrifice
is self-fulfillment, a "becomingness" and not a "ceasing to be":

> The vulgar conception of sacrifice is of an act of painful self-im-
> molation, austere self-mortification, difficult self-effacement; this
> kind of sacrifice may go even as far as self-mutilation and self-
> torture. . . . But the true essence of sacrifice is not self-immolation,
> it is self-giving; its object not self-effacement, but self-fulfillment; its
> method not self-mortification, but a greater life; not self-mutilation,
> but a transformation of our natural human parts into divine mem-
> bers; not self-torture, but a passage from a lesser satisfaction to a
> greater Ananda. There is only one thing painful in the beginning
> to a raw or turbid part of the surface nature; it is the indispensable
> discipline demanded, the denial necessary for the merging of the
> incomplete ego. . . . Our sacrifice is not a giving without any return
> or any fruitful acceptance from the other side; it is an interchange
> between the embodied soul and conscious Nature in us and the
> eternal Spirit. For even though no return is demanded, yet there is
> the knowledge deep within us that a marvelous return is inevitable.
> The soul knows that it does not give itself to God in vain; claiming
> nothing, it yet receives the infinite riches of the Divine Power and
> Presence.[57]

The two movements, aspiration from below and descent from
above, must meet. Where do they meet? They meet in the gnostic
individual. The purpose of the evolution is the creation of the
gnostic individual, indeed, a *race* of gnostic beings. Who is the
gnostic individual? What is the nature of his transformation? How
does he act? These are important questions in the philosophy of
the integral Yoga. The appearance of gnostic individuals in history is a link between Time and Eternity. Śri Aurobindo says concerning the gnostic consciousness:

> The gnostic life will be an inner life in which the antinomy of the
> inner and the outer, the self and the world, will have been cured
> and exceeded. The gnostic being will have indeed an inmost exist-
> ence in which he is alone with God, one with the Eternal, self-
> plunged into the depths of the Infinite, in communion with its
> heights and its luminous abysses of secrecy; nothing will be able to
> disturb or to invade these depths or bring him down from the sum-
> mits, neither the world's contents nor his action nor all that is

[57] *Ibid.,* p. 71.

around him. This is the transcendence aspect of the spiritual life and it is necessary for the freedom of the spirit; for otherwise the identity in Nature with the world would be a binding limitation and not a free identity. But at the same time God-love and the delight of God will be the heart's expression of that inner communion and oneness, and that delight and love will expand itself to embrace all existence. The peace of God within will be extended in the gnostic experience of the universe into a universal calm of equality not merely passive but dynamic, a calm of freedom in oneness dominating all that meets it, tranquilizing all that enters into it, imposing its law of peace on the supramental being's relations with the world in which he is living. The inner oneness, the inner communion, will attend him in all his acts and enter into his relations with others, who will not be to him others but selves of himself in the one existence, his own universal existence. It is this poise and freedom in the spirit that will enable him to take all life into himself while still remaining the spiritual self, and to embrace even the world of Ignorance without himself entering into Ignorance.[58]

The perfection of integral Yoga will come when each man is able to follow his own path of yoga, pursuing the development of his own nature; for *freedom is the essence and the final law of integral Yoga.* By integral Yoga we not only seek the Infinite, but we call upon the Infinite to unfold himself in human life: the final doctrine of integral Yoga is an infinite liberty in the receptive human soul. Swami Vivekananda, pointing to the unity of all religions, said that the perfect state of essential unity would come when each man has his own religion; when, not bound by sect or traditional form he follows the free self-adaptation of his nature in its relation to the Supreme. *To turn one's soul toward the Divine: this change of life is "conversion" and not a change from one religious sect or faith to another.*

The following conversation between an American and the head of an institution of nondualist *Vedānta* may be found interesting:

"Why must it be," impatiently demanded an earnest American tourist, "that you will not convert other peoples to Hinduism? You have such a beautiful religion, and yet you keep so many struggling souls out of it. If you say 'yes' I will be first to become a Hindu!"

[58] Aurobindo, *The Life Divine* (Calcutta, 1944), II, 835-36.

"But why," came the counterquestion, "do you want to change your religion? What is wrong with Christianity?"

Taken aback, but not daunted, the tourist said: "I cannot say what is wrong, but it has not given me satisfaction."

"Indeed, it is unfortunate," was the reply, "but tell me honestly whether you have given it a real chance. Have you fully understood the religion of Christ and lived according to it? Have you been a true Christian and yet found the religion wanting?"

"I am afraid I cannot say that, Sir."

"Then we advise you to go and be a true Christian first. Live truly by the word of the Lord, and if even then you feel unfulfilled it will be time to consider what should be done. *What you must change is not your faith but your life.*" [59]

Summary and Conclusion

I have indicated in this essay some of the major ideas characteristic of Indian thought which have found confirmation in the living continuity of contemporary Indian experience. They are the following:

(a) The idea of *sama-darśana*, "perception of equality," which has its basis in the nondualism of the Upaniṣads. *Sama-darśana* is the perception of the divine in all existence.

They ask me, if my ceaseless wanderings are part of a religious pilgrimage, what is the God that I worship and why do I not go to the particular place where I may find Him? But I say that my God does not reside at any one place or point. My God resides in every human heart; He pervades the entire space and every object however small or big.[60]

This idea unites mysticism with common sense, if I may say so, and makes the *Vedānta* more a philosophy of the masses than a doctrine of the intellectuals.

(b) The idea of *Yajna*, which is an act of self-giving or sacrifice; it is the basic truth in Creation; it has ontological and ethicosocial significance; it governs human relations and social order, and is

[59] *Harijan,* November 21, 1953. Italics mine.
[60] Vinoba Bhave, *Harijan,* January 23, 1954.

the gospel of work in the contemporary Indian social renaissance or revolution under Ācharya Vinoba Bhave.

(c) "The central doctrine of mysticism," says Dean Inge, "is not that we can see God only in a state of swoon, but that we can see only what we are." [61] What are we? What can we become, and not only, what can we *know?* are questions to which Indian thought has sought answers in man's immediate experience, *anubhava.* Neither logic nor authority but experience and verification is the last word of Indian thought and its criterion of truth and reality. *Sa yo ha vai tat paramam brahma veda brahmaiva bhavati:* "He, verily, who knows the Supreme *Brahman* becomes *Brahman* himself." [62] To know is to be; "to be" is "to be free"; to be free is to be free from "the bonds of death *before* death."

Mysticism is the discovery of this freedom or salvation in man's immediate experience. It is the expression of the fundamental urge of man "to be." There is nothing mysterious and hidden in this urge. So the *Brihad-Āraṇyaka Upaniṣad,* in giving expression to this urge, "From death lead me to immortality," *mṛtyor mā amṛtam gamaya,* adds: "There is nothing here that is hidden": *nātra tirohitam ivāsti.*[63]

[61] James Hastings (ed.), *Ency. of Religion and Ethics* (New York, 1917), IX, 316.

[62] Radhakrishnan, *op. cit., Muṇḍaka Upaniṣad,* III.2.9.

[63] *Ibid., Brihad-āranyaka Upaniṣad,* I.3.28.

✣ X ✣

MYSTICISM AND EXISTENTIALISM[1]

NEWTON P. STALLKNECHT

THERE ARE MANY VARIETIES of existentialism as there are many types of mysticism. In this essay, at the risk of over-simplification, we shall consider only those aspects of the two traditions that seem at times to merge with one another or to stand in marked contrast.

In so far as mysticism tends toward pantheism and the surrender of individuality, it will encounter little sympathy from the existentialist. On the other hand, the existentialist often follows the practice of the mystic in seeking intuitive apprehension of features of reality not usually recognized by the theorist.

Existentialism, as a way of thought and experience, centers upon the human individual's sense of his own unique reality primarily as an agent capable of free and responsible decision and commitment. The unorthodox Danish theologian, Sören Kierkegaard, recognized in the act of religious faith a commitment of this sort, whereby the individual declares himself as accepting a certain orientation and as cherishing certain values. Such a profound commitment can be made only in a spirit of absolute sincerity, in "fear and trembling," in anxiety or anguish, as the believer asks himself whether this decision is a genuine one, accepted for its own sake and not motivated by some desire for respectability or mere peace of mind. In such experience, anxiety may be an index of the sincerity that supports genuine individuality. In recent years existentialist philosophers have pointed out that what Kierkegaard had to say about religious commitment may be applied to many other decisions by which the individual characterizes his existence.

[1] I have incorporated in this essay several passages taken from my reviews of Marcel, Wahl, and Chaix-Ruy published in *The Review of Metaphysics*, VII (June, 1954); VIII (September, 1954, June, 1955).

Human individuality takes shape in a world of intersubjective communication, co-operation, and conflict. Our relation to other people, recognized as other selves or in a certain sense as genuine alter egos is often more important than our equally unavoidable relation to things, and even to ideas. Thus the existentialist is fascinated by the insight that supports our use of personal pronouns. The existence indicated by the words "I," "you," and "we" is inseparable from the self-maintaining activity of conscious life. Here existence is manifest not in our use of "is" or "are" as the copula of formal logic but in our recognition, often intuitive, of a spontaneity that shapes itself as a center of freedom and responsibility.

Responsibility indicates not only a moral consistency but also an ability to communicate intelligibly and to make one's motives clear to other people. Responsibility is intersubjective. We predict the movement of things; we question and approve or disapprove the decisions of people. In doing so, we admit their existence as persons, capable of raising the same question about themselves and even about us. To discern such existence is to sense the presence of originality or sincerity as distinct from its strictly third person opposite, thinghood, and again as distinct from the many counterfeits of authentic existence present in all forms of "bad faith" and self-deception that characterize the corruption of human consciousness. The corrupt consciousness refuses to comprehend or avoids comprehending its own actions and thus fails to consider their nature and consequences. Thus, while things are wholly lacking in original or authentic existence, corrupt consciousness caricatures or disqualifies its spontaneity, being an existence that denies or conceals itself, thus distorting or destroying intersubjective life through which responsibility flourishes.

The human spirit awakens or first comes to consciousness in a complex situation at once natural, social, and historical in structure, that at first largely determines its attitude. The spirit discovers itself as arbitrarily at the mercy of a world it never made and cannot comprehend, but which it must accept. It is not surprising that in the early stages of this awakening human consciousness sometimes abases itself before its world, eager to propitiate the forces that constitute its environment and too willing to renounce what measure of freedom it may have achieved. At this stage, the group usually overwhelms the individual for whom an independence of decision seems unthinkable, responsibility being absorbed in a sense of social obligation, supporting tradition.

The attitude of many recent existentialists may be described as the diametric opposite of this primitive consciousness. For these philosophers, the individual can in no way escape responsibility or renounce his freedom; and, in trying to do so, he can only caricature without transforming his life as a human being. Between these two extremes lies a long development, a history that some followers of Hegel, recalling their master's great work, the *Phenomenology of the Spirit,* would describe as the proper subject of philosophical study. Only gradually, passing through many stages of self-interpretation, does our consciousness succeed in overcoming its initial predicament, declaring itself at last as an autonomous agent or responsible individual, capable of self-direction based on self-knowledge. The human existence or self-realization that emerges stands in spectacular contrast to the life of plants and animals and to the endurance of inanimate things.

This contrast stands for existentialist thinkers as the central object of their attention. Philosophy is concerned primarily with the elucidation of human existence. Such elucidation is by no means purely a matter of rational analysis. It begins with what we might call the intuitive margins of our intersubjective consciousness. Here we come upon insights that are usually not recorded in traditional terminology and whose content often lies beyond the reach of popular idiom. At this point, the existentialist and the mystic have much in common, since both are often concerned with the ineffable. This aspect of existentialist thought is well illustrated by Professor Jean Wahl of the Sorbonne in his recent *Traité de Métaphysique:*

> . . . an immediate vision remains the goal of the philosopher. The criticism of Hegel was based on an analysis of language. According to him the now and the here, being always changing, are only ab-

stract ideas. But he did not take account of the fact that the sentence containing the words "now" and "here" points to a reality beyond itself, and, as we have said, that thought is always directed toward things. Hegel's criticism is destructive of the intellectual now and here, but not the now and here as they are felt, which language can describe only imperfectly. From the imperfections of language we cannot infer anything about the so-called imperfections of reality.[2]

Hegel's adverse critique of immediacy, so prominent in the argument of his *Phenomenology*, is based on an analysis of language. Wahl insists that we must not let language, "taken literally," come between us and the real. He would seem to seek an absolute awareness that, like Bergson's intuition, dispenses with symbols.

It is true, of course, that through dialectical criticism we may sometimes sharpen our ideas, supplementing each term by its contrary. But this process is an unending one, and we must learn to look beyond words and definitions if only to distinguish these from reality, if only to insist that our ideas are *not* reality. Such extralinguistic vision is a grasp of the immediate. It appears almost as a return to the immediate, which it would seem has all along been present to us, hardly noticed behind the screen of language. The thing-in-itself seems to lurk behind the phenomena of linguistic presentation. We might almost say that the phenomenal order is our way of talking about the real. Since conventions of verbalization color observation as well as theory, this extralinguistic reality is often ignored.

Existentialist insight is, however, chiefly directed toward the life of the conscious individual recognized as an activity of self-realization and self-maintenance. Existentialism springs from an intuition of our freedom. The very existence of the individual is seen as concentrated in acts of self-determination whereby the individual chooses or conditions his own character as a responsible being who is willing to recognize himself as the author of this or that statement or action. Speaking more technically, personal existence is a self-determination of essence or character. Thus in

[2] *Traité de Métaphysique* (Paris, 1953), p. 23.

recent European philosophy we have seen the scholastic concepts
of essence and existence, in various reinterpretations, once again
occupying a central position both in speculative theory and in
the phenomenology of our daily experience.[3] Some sense of this
contrast is always with us as we come to self-consciousness and as
we orient ourselves in our world. But we rarely interpret this insight very precisely in practical life; and when we attempt to do
so in philosophical language difficulties multiply on every hand.
We are often tempted to avoid these embarrassments by resorting
to specious simplifications. So motivated, a student may summarize the essentialism, say, of Spinoza and the existentialism of
Sartre, in order to set in easy but too obvious contrast opposed
interpretations of existence and essence. At first glance such opposition seems enlightening. We have, to put it very simply,
libertarianism versus determinism, and a neat if drastic option
seems available. For Sartre, finite human existence shapes its own
essence: human nature is, briefly, what we make it. The existential
cogito, despite the shock of finding itself in a world and intimately
entangled with the human body, is its own master and even a sort
of paradoxical *ens a se.* Here we are faced with a creative inde-
terminism, a transcendental subjectivism, "subjectivism" becoming once more an honorific term, whereby human choice and self-
commitment actually create human nature and determine a
"world" of fact and value through a process of selective recognition. We may then put this philosophy, although somewhat
arbitrarily, in diametric opposition to Spinoza's theory of man.
Spinoza saw all transiency, including human action and passion,
as dependent upon a fixed nature or order of things from which
all properties and events, including apparent accidents and con-
tingencies, may be thought to follow. In such a scheme of things,
human freedom is interpreted as an effective knowledge of our
circumstances and causation. Self-creation, or self-causation, is
reserved for God alone, if indeed even for him; and the proper
attitude for finite man is that of enlightened acquiescence. Now,

[3] See Jules Chaix-Ruy, *Les dimensions de l'être et du temps* (Paris, 1953),
where these concepts are presented both systematically and historically with
reference to such writers as Lavelle, Jaspers, Abbagano, and Marcel.

in both of the above interpretations essence appears as the direct object of a definition—as, properly speaking, a real *definiendum* —and existence as some sort of process or activity either exemplifying, perhaps "following from," the reality defined or, quite otherwise, actually creating it through the implications of the self-commitment which characterizes human nature. These extreme statements of freedom and necessity are hardly consistent with our sense of life and of action according to which freedom and necessity always qualify one another. Furthermore, this antithesis involves us in an oversimplification that requires us to choose abruptly between essentialism and existentialism. After all, existence without or prior to essence is a puzzling concept, and on the other hand, a determining essence prior to or "above" our actual decision would seem to be a target ready-made for the exercise of Ockham's razor.

To avoid this blunt and embarrassing alternative seems to be the goal of much recent philosophy—and especially of continental European thought. It becomes apparent at once that these problems cannot be separated from our experience and interpretation of process and duration, of time and change, and of our place within or with reference to them. Here mystic and existentialist have an interest in common.

The relation of essence to existence in human life is a unique one, quite different from that to be found elsewhere among non-human or subhuman beings. This contrast involves a description of man's relation to time and to change. Human nature is subject to change, or better, man subjects himself to change. "Chez nous l'essence est in fieri." We are reminded of Sartre's "Faire et en faisant se faire," although, as we shall soon see, we need not think of the initiative as lying wholly with our existence, as opposed to our essence. After all, an existence capable of transforming essence must have a structure of its own and a *modus operandi*. Even the freest choice is "structured." This would seem to be true even if our creative self-realization in some way embraces or contains nonbeing.

But time and duration are by no means always a matrix of self-realization. Time may appear as a prison or booby trap, as the ultimate condition of human frustration. "At ego in tempora dissilui." Man can lose himself in time, as Augustine knew, and forfeit the "authenticity" of his being by doing so. We are reminded of T. S. Eliot's lines in "Burnt Norton":

> Time past and time future
> Allow but a little consciousness.
> To be conscious is not to be in time.

The unexamined and undisciplined life of the dilettante or the worldling is distracted, even dismembered, by fears, regrets, and ambitions. It is scattered through the reaches of time, lacking even the autonomic quality of the Cyrenaic's *habeo non habeor* that clings to the *monochronos hedoné,* the isolated pleasure, of the present moment. In such distraction, past and future encroach upon our present. There is no moment of self-orientation, of resolution, or of dedication. There is only a "pursuit of interests" —one objective after another, a flux of apparent "ends," some of which appear as unrealized in a past of frustrations; others in a remote future. In such a life there is no substantial evaluation on the part of the individual and there often results an indifference or "power vacuum" of the spirit. Here is that

> Inoperancy of the world of spirit

of which Eliot speaks,

> . . . while the world moves
> In appetency, on its metalled ways
> Of time past and time future.

Here we have only a *de facto* or (almost) a subhuman essence. Human character when so distracted and so dissipated lacks authenticity or genuine originality. Indeed, it lacks substance or self-directive stability. We might add as a historical comment that Hume gives a fairly satisfactory account of such a pseudo-selfhood and that his philosophy—a world view for those still deep in Plato's cave—presents, both as an epistemology and as a theory of value, an interpretation of things characteristic of one who, unlike Augustine, can *cheerfully* lose himself in time and find reason properly enough the "slave of the passions." Such a life is carried along or thrown about in a flux of events. It is so deeply involved therein that no lasting comprehension of another state of affairs is possible. For such an attitude, reality is made of things and things of events, standing like points on a curve. But there remains a vast and fundamental difference between an event and a decision or a commitment. The moment of sincere and responsible decision is no ordinary, natural event. It is not a moment *in* or *of* the flux; although of course relevant to the world of events, such decision "stands above" change even more clearly than veridical memory or prediction. It is certainly not to be included in the continuum of space-time, say, as a flash of light is included. The order of an "objective" [4] sequence open to perception must not be confused with the "time" of a moment of resolution. We may even say that they belong to different "levels of time." On the level of human commitment, volition stands as an active interpretation of past and future. Without this significance, it would lose its status as an act of resolution. It would remain merely an event. We might comment that in this sense an act of commitment stands, perhaps like the option described in Plato's "Myth of Er," without or above a purely sequential time, i.e., time as apparent to those in the cave. But man is not meant for the cave. He is called upon to ascend from lower to higher levels since in the beginning his existence cannot escape inauthenticity: man is born in the cave, but in his ascent from the cave human nature takes shape, assuming an authenticity as it develops. Man is not born free but he is privileged to achieve a freedom of his own.

Such freedom cannot be exhaustively described although it can be felt as a sense of responsibility.

If we were to think theoretically about the two words "I become," we should soon lose the meaning of each. Who is this I? And if I am I, how can I become? But there is a practical solution, which consists in the construction of ourselves and at the same time the destruction of ourselves, because the one does not take place without the other. We have to become our Being and to be our Becoming, uniting these two elements by our works, by our oath and promise,

---

[4] "Objectif, c'est ce qui correspond à un object réel et effectivement mesurable" (Chaix-Ruy, *op. cit.*, p. 126).

which, as the philosophers Alain and Sartre have insisted, reveal our will to constitute our stability within our Becoming. By our oath, as Sartre says, we link our future with our present and our past.[5]

We may say that "our personality centers around the free act." Here in our awareness of our own existence we find an intuitive reconciliation of our participation in the world of things and events and of our limited but genuine dominion over our own lives. In a sense, we *are* our past lives, and our freedom requires us to answer for a past while we lay claim to a future as also our own. The decisive present holds past and future in an existential unity. In the moment of commitment our human decision reconciles, or shall we say, realizes possibility and necessity, freedom and determinism. We remain in our world—the world that has begotten us and from which we cannot escape—but it is all the more our world because in action we leave *our* mark upon it.

> . . . Our admiration for the achievement of Van Gogh and even of Cézanne cannot be separated from our feeling that we are in the presence of their personal effort, as expressed in the kind of brush strokes they employ, and we feel them as men at the same time that we admire them as painters.[6]

Existence, in this sense, is freedom, but freedom incarnate in a world which it accepts and transforms however briefly and modestly.

> The metaphysical pride of the idealist is replaced by a realistic humility, for which man is open to the world and the world to man: so that man and the world contribute to one another's formation—man constituting the possibility of the world, the world constituting the supporting or substantial reality of man. But such realistic humility does not mean renunciation or any lack of courage. For man, to recognize his place in the world, such as it is, is an act of courage.[7]

Here human essence and existence are made to stand in intimate relation that seems to render them internal to one another. Human existence is the effort, or moment of commitment, of which human essence is the complete significance or intention.

[5] Jean Wahl, *Traité de Métaphysique*, p. 49.
[6] Wahl, *Philosopher's Way* (New York, 1948), p. 49.
[7] *Traité de Métaphysique*, p. 562.

We come to ourselves as beings living within a world of restless movement. As our self-realization is completed we distinguish ourselves as existing within this world and yet in a sense as distinct from it. Thus we may be said to transcend the world without leaving it. Were I not in the world I could not transcend it, and were I not capable of some degree of such transcendence, I could not achieve the detachment necessary to recognize that I exist in a world of things, of events, and of other people. I would not, indeed, distinguish myself from the world around me, and in this case *I* would hardly exist at all.

Our being in this world may, as an experience, conflict with our first assertion of individual agency or transcendence of an initial situation. It is almost as if the world, including our social environment, considered as a group to which the individual *belongs,* resists our self-assertion and even threatens it most effectively through its enormous indifference to the reality of the individual who seems to declare himself in vain. At this moment, the individual faces the mighty "happenstance" or arbitrary absoluteness of a scheme of things that does not "exist" but smothers existence in its brutal sublimity. Our attitude becomes one of awe-stricken indignation or helpless refusal, even, at times, of disgust. Such repudiation is well known to Sartre and is found frequently among the romantic poets, as in Coleridge's *Ancient Mariner,* "alone on a wide, wide sea," with "water everywhere nor any drop to drink." Coleridge's image of the slimy water snakes reminds us of at least one passage from Sartre's *Nausea:*

> Had I dreamed of this enormous presence? It was there, in the garden, toppled down into the trees, all soft, sticky, soiling everything, all thick, a jelly. And I was inside, I with the garden. I was frightened, furious, I thought it was so stupid, so out of place, I hated this ignoble mess. Mounting up, mounting up as high as the sky, spilling over, filling everything with its gelatinous slither, and I could see depths upon depths of it reaching far beyond the limits of the garden, the houses, and Bouville, as far as the eye could reach. I was no longer in Bouville, I was nowhere, I was floating. I was not surprised, I knew it was the World, the naked World suddenly revealing itself, and I choked with rage at this gross, absurd being. You couldn't even wonder where all that sprang from, or how

it was that a world came into existence, rather than nothingness. It didn't make sense, the World was everywhere, in front, behind. . . . There had never been a moment in which it could not have existed. That was what worried me: of course there was no *reason* for this flowing lava to exist. *But it was impossible* for it not to exist. It was unthinkable: to imagine nothingness you had to be there already, in the midst of the World, eyes wide open and alive; nothingness was only an idea in my head, an existing idea floating in this immensity: this nothingness had not come *before* existence, it was an existence like any other and appeared after many others. I shouted "filth! what rotten filth!" and shook myself to get rid of this sticky filth, but it held fast and there was so much, tons and tons, of existence, endless: I stifled at the depths of this immense weariness. And then suddenly the park emptied as through a great hole, the World disappeared as it had come, or else I woke up—in any case, I saw no more of it; nothing was left but the yellow earth around me, out of which dead branches rose upward.[8]

We may also cite Heidegger's illuminating remark that in boredom we are aware of Being as a whole, a total universe that offers us nothing. Such utterances may remind the student of an inverted mysticism that apprehends reality as a prison house. Here the great intuition of the mystic presents itself without religious ecstasy or fulfillment. An awakened self-consciousness isolates itself, condemning the world and all that's in it.

> The sky and the sea, and the sea and the sky
> Lay like a load on my weary eye. . . .

Such an experience, a sort of "dark night of the soul," is known to many mystics, although the greatest of them succeed in passing beyond it toward a communion with God or Nature that the existentialist is less likely to achieve. The latter is by temperament bound to resist a voluntary surrender or loss of self within that infinite ocean or desert of divine being that so many mystics accept as the origin and underlying reality of all things. Indeed, for some existentialists, even if such a monstrous and indeterminate reservoir of creative power were accepted as real, it would not compare in value to the humblest center of finite conscious-

---

[8] Jean-Paul Sartre, *Nausea,* tr. Lloyd Alexander (Norfolk, Conn., 1949), pp. 180-81. In this passage *existence* refers to sheer or arbitrary "facticity."

ness, seeking to declare itself in face of a world. Or we may consider the position of Sartre who argues that an eternal God, secure above the fluctuations of becoming, cannot be a center of conscious decision. Consciousness requires an open future and the presence of an otherness not wholly subject to our will. For Sartre, if such a God existed, his fiat would determine good and evil in advance of our experience. This, as a left-wing existentialist, he will not accept. For him the human self awakens to a situation, or, we might say, a predicament, but subject to no external authority and without the support or mediation of God, man, or Nature. Thus the individual, even in the moment of profoundest commitment that lies beneath the *sic et non* of superficial deliberation, stands alone.

> . . . For a human being, to *be* is to choose himself; nothing comes to him either from without or from within himself that he can receive or accept. He is wholly and helplessly at the mercy of the unendurable necessity to make himself be, even in the smallest details of his existence.[9]
>
> . . . My freedom is the unique foundation of values. And since I am the being by virtue of whom values exist, nothing—absolutely nothing—can justify me in adopting this or that value or scale of values. As the unique basis of the existence of values, I am totally unjustifiable. And my freedom is in anguish at finding that it is the baseless basis of values.[10]
>
> . . . Life has no meaning *a priori* . . . it's up to you to give it a meaning, and value is nothing else but the meaning that you choose.[11]

Sartre's philosophy might be compared to an inverted Christianity, for which the fall of man is to be interpreted as a liberation and a fulfillment; or to an inverted classicism according to which *hubris* is the only virtue; again in quasi-trinitarian terms to a revolt of the Spirit who refuses to admit any dependence upon Father or Son. From the Father proceeds creative power, but the Spirit is free only in so far as it creates for itself. The Son embodies the wisdom and the way of life, eternally begotten by the

[9] Sartre, *Etre et le Néant,* Part IV, Chapter 1, Section 1, quoted from Gabriel Marcel, *The Philosophy of Existence,* tr. Manya Harari (London, 1948), p. 57.

[10] *Ibid.,* Part I, Chapter I, Section 5. See *The Philosophy of Existence,* p. 63.

[11] *Existentialism,* tr. Bernard Frechtman (New York, 1947), p. 58.

Father. But the Spirit can profit only by wisdom that it has itself derived from experience. It can gain nothing by seeking assistance. It must help itself. The world may present the human Spirit with problems and difficulties. It may supply the occasion of action. But the decision and the action belong wholly to the Spirit itself.

Sartre has labeled his existentialism as "atheistic." He has really gone beyond atheism and repudiated all forms of piety that look to "something not ourselves." The self-surrender that stands at the threshold of a mystical religion can be for Sartre only a gesture of bad faith whereby we seek to avoid the full burden of a responsibility exclusively our own. The sincerity by which we recognize an inescapable responsibility, including the anxiety or even anguish with which we at last accept our lonely situation, must take the place of the faith and hope that supported our ancestors. Nor may we follow the romantic poets who extol a "return to nature" and a loss of self-consciousness in a Dionysiac surrender to life. The latter constitutes no more than an effort to ignore our own existence.

There are, however, other types of existentialism. It is indeed possible to speak of an existentialist piety and in some cases of an existentialist religion that cultivates a mystical insight. Thus certain existentialists quite willingly emphasize a proposition that seems to them obvious, that we do not by our own fiat create our freedom out of nothing. Thus in opposition to Sartre we come upon Marcel, Buber, and Jaspers, each of whom undertakes to avoid Sartre's tendency to identify existence with isolation. For all these thinkers, the individual who maintains his freedom does so not through an isolated or gratuitous gesture of his own but through discovering and realizing a value or ideal latent in his cultural and historical situation and making this the center of his self-realization. The achievement of freedom involves recognition and acceptance of a destiny, imperfectly reflected in our religious and philosophical traditions. Such self-realization is supported by an intuitive insight not easily recorded in academic or scientific language. One of the primary duties of an existentialist philosopher is to record and elucidate such insight. This can be done only by resort to language that will be considered unjustifiably figurative or metaphorical by many students of philosophy.

Let us begin with Marcel's repudiation of Sartre:

> *So soon as man denies to himself that he is a created being,* a double peril faces him: on the one hand he will be led—and this is exactly what we see in Sartre's type of existentialism—to claim for himself a kind of *self-dependence* which caricatures that of the Deity. He will be led, that is, to consider himself as a being who makes himself and *is* only what he makes of himself; for there is nobody who can destroy his self-sufficiency; similarly there is no gift which can be made to that sufficiency; a being conceived as Sartre conceives man is utterly incapable of receiving anything. But from another point of view, and yet in a closely connected way, the man who conceives himself as Sartre conceives man will be led to think of himself as a sort of waste product of a universe which is, for that matter, an inconceivable universe—so that we see such a man, at the same time and for the same set of reasons, exalting and abasing himself beyond all just measure.[12]

In contrast, Marcel speaks with a generous admiration of the Stoic belief in an "inalienable inner sovereignty, an absolute possession of the self by the self," but he recognizes that such an autonomy can flourish only in a soil that will nourish it; and the soil, say, of a totalitarian system of education will not foster such "inner freedom." Both Stoic and Existentialist must recognize the finitude and dependency of human beings, creatures capable of freedom, but by no means assured of it or in any sense *condemned* to be free.

Freedom is a gift, an opportunity, that many are not able to recognize or to accept. The thoughtful free man knows only too well that but for favorable circumstances, perhaps but for the "grace of God," he might never have found himself. With his freedom his life is put into his charge to commit and dispose. His life then becomes his own. And as this takes place, a distinction appears between his life and his being. My being is the freedom which presides over my life. It is inner selfhood. Thus, the "grace" which offers me freedom offers me a reality that transcends my

---

[12] Gabriel Marcel, *Man Against Mass Society* (Chicago, 1952), p. 50. (Italics Marcel's.)

"life." Freedom belongs to the spirit—is, indeed, the spirit itself—and cannot be reduced wholly to biological or economic terms. Without freedom there is no humanity and man is reduced to the status of a thing or a machine. He becomes a "gadget" to be evaluated purely in terms of efficiency and output and, properly enough, to be scrapped once the necessary repairs become too expensive. Without freedom we have only the "mass man" who is to be considered merely as a producer and a consumer without individual quality or personal worth, whose "behavior" is the proper subject of the propagandist's conditioning. It is the capacity for freedom which constitutes each human being an end in himself, for whose sake machines and gadgets properly exist. In recent years we have witnessed the denial of freedom and know, to our shame and sorrow, that the above considerations are by no means purely academic.

The gift of freedom is the gift of a higher selfhood. As we become free, we grow in ontological stature. Marcel quotes Keats: The world is a "vale of soul-making." Such insight, like that of Plato's "Myth of Er," transcends the discursive problem stating and problem "solving" of the systematic philosopher. Marcel reminds us of Bergson when he hints that there can be no "theory" of freedom. Freedom presents us with a "mystery" rather than a problem. In any case, we must penetrate the mystery, i.e., we must clarify our experience or vision of freedom before we can formulate problems. As a genuine mystery, the sense of freedom is inescapable; we feel and assume its existence throughout our lives. As Samuel Johnson seems to have believed, all our intersubjective experience reveals the importance of freedom, although no theoretical statement can do it justice. Freedom is not reducible to a formula, it does not center upon a scheme of behavior contemplated in advance. There is, strictly speaking, no technique of freedom. Furthermore, in Marcel's mind freedom is not a Kantian autonomy. We cannot reduce it to acceptance of a maxim. Thus, we do not "give the law" to ourselves. The good faith or fidelity of the free man is a richer thing than any strict self-control. It is a sense of devotion, which takes spontaneously an intersubjective form:

Something has been entrusted to us, so that we are not only responsible toward ourselves, but toward an active and superior principle—and how it goes against my inclinations to use such a disgustingly abstract word! [13]

Martin Buber offers a more traditional interpretation than does Marcel in his effort to clarify our sense of freedom and obligation. Buber prefers language more emphatically anthropomorphic than that of Marcel. For Buber, human existence is most clearly manifest, perhaps we should say realized, by a consciousness that looks toward a source of evaluation beyond itself, as in prayer or religious meditation.

> . . . do we not discover, in the depth of any genuine solitude, that even beyond all social existence—nay, precisely in this realm—there is a conflict between good and evil, between fulfillment and failure to fulfill the purpose embodied in us, in this individual being? And yet I am constitutionally incapable of conceiving of myself as the ultimate source of moral approval or disapproval of myself, as surety for the absoluteness that I, to be sure, do not possess, but nevertheless imply with respect to this yes or no. The encounter with the original voice, the original source of yes or no, cannot be replaced by any self-encounter.[14]

This "original source of yes or no," this center of authority, may be invoked or addressed more easily than described. It stands to us in the second person as essentially a "thou," whose voice has entered the depth of our consciousness and calls upon us, not to seek security but to pursue freedom, as freedom is made clear to us in our prayers and meditations. Marcel's "active and superior principle" is translated into more traditional terms reminding us of Wordsworth's "Ode to Duty." Thus in the end our primary responsibility is directed not toward our fellow men but toward the God who speaks to us, as it were, from within ourselves, and without whose voice we are not wholly and truly ourselves.

Martin Heidegger stands closer to Marcel and Buber than to Sartre although he is not ready to employ the anthropomorphism that these writers find helpful. Being is achieved in our acts of

13 Marcel, *Being and Having*, tr. Katharine Farrer (London, 1949), p. 15.
14 Martin Buber, *Eclipse of God* (New York, 1952), pp. 27-28.

resolute self-commitment; but it is, in a sense, a gift that can be accepted only through a courageous effort. Our free existence, so long as we succeed in maintaining it as free, is the dwelling place of a Being that we feel under obligation to cherish. The commonplace daily life of busy concern for passing detail conceals the truth of Being and subjects us to an inauthentic or fundamentally irresponsible participation in superficialities, which we share with an anonymous public whose dicta seem so authoritative, especially when clothed in a mass medium of communication. It would seem that only the great poets can succeed in recording the conditions under which authentic reality is revealed to us. Heidegger turns to Hölderlin and to Rilke, who urge us to stand in expectation of a revelation denied to our present culture. We should not say with Nietzsche that "God is dead" but rather that in our own age of superficial distractions the gods are silent. We live in exile, but we are still somehow able to recognize our exile for what it is. Thus Heidegger's philosophy stands, so to speak, just on the hither side of mystical insight.

The student of philosophy, trained in academic circles, may well prefer Karl Jaspers' rendering of the sense of freedom since he avoids the anthropomorphic figures that tend to dominate the speculative imagination of both Marcel and Buber without retreating into the mysterious and laconic reticence of Heidegger. Jaspers will not tolerate the isolationism of Sartre. "Human existence," he insists, "does not create itself." Our actions are ours only in and through our total environment and especially in and through our historical traditions whose meaning may become clear to us only as our actions participate in them. In moments of creative freedom our human existence becomes a realization of ourselves not in isolation but as an expression of a world situation that we have made our own.

Jaspers' terminology is difficult and we shall accordingly quote in a free paraphrase from his *Reason and Existence:* "Human existence is (or successfully identifies itself with its) encompassing reality, taken not in the sense of a vast expanse including all horizons, but rather in the sense of an underlying origin or condition of selfhood and freedom. Without this, the vast expanse of

Being would be no more than a desert of thinghood without meaning or intention."

We are truly aware of our human existence as we reflect directly upon our acts of decision and self-commitment. Our understanding of ourselves is rather an act of reflective self-enjoyment than of discursive description.

Here Jaspers approaches the mystics in inviting us to bring all our powers of intuition toward a comprehension of our freedom. He seems to say that only in a freedom so comprehended do we achieve that fullness of being that deserves the name of human existence.

> When human existence understands itself, it is not like my understanding of another, nor the sort of understanding whose contents can be abstracted from the person understanding, nor a sort of "looking at"; rather this understanding is a resolution, an origin which first declares itself in its own self-clarification. It is not like sharing in something else, but is at once the understanding and the being of what is understood. (It is decision and creative action.) It is not understanding through universals, but moves above such understanding in the medium of spirit to become an understanding without any generalization in the absolute present, in deed, in love, and in every form of absolute consciousness. It is the difference between the love of another, which I recognize but yet never really understand, and my own love, which I understand because I am that love. Or, in other words, the difference between understanding other things by empathy as process or experience, and understanding myself as unique . . .[15]

We may observe that the existentialist philosophers have found in human existence an object of attention and a center of meditation, a target of both intuition and theoretical speculation, a meeting place of value and reality. They bring toward its elucidation all the energy and all the skill that earlier philosophers directed toward the notion of deity. In so far as the observation and evaluation upon which their speculation is based is often of an intuitive nature, they may be compared to the mystics. The pattern of their thought often reminds us vividly of the latter. For both mystic

[15] I have paraphrased a passage in *Reason and Existence,* translated by William Earle. See Walter Kaufmann, *Existentialism from Dostoevsky to Sartre* (New York, 1957), p. 194.

and existentialist, philosophy is essentially an effort to find words for an insight that is usually deemed incommunicable. The great traditions of mystical literature embody the insights of the unusually gifted, the saints and seers of religion and philosophy. The existentialists have turned their attention toward an insight that is more generally accessible and yet quite as difficult to interpret: our sense of agency and responsibility.

⚙ XI ⚙

SOME PHILOSOPHICAL IMPLICATIONS
OF MYSTICISM

ALFRED P. STIERNOTTE

I have been obliged to speak of philosophy as a satisfaction of what may be called the mystical side of our nature.

F. H. BRADLEY [1]

There is a sound and a dangerous mysticism. The sound variety is an essential ingredient in all religion; it is not too much to say that it is the vital ingredient of religion, without which religion is a thing of forms. . . . The dangerous form of mysticism is that in which the worshipper is lost in the adoration of God, and God becomes an infinite abyss of negatives, an abstraction which, in purporting to be the secret of reality, is in fact attenuated into the indescribable.

SAMUEL ALEXANDER [2]

WILLIAM JAMES in evaluating the validity of mysticism in *Varieties of Religious Experience* expresses in his own picturesque manner the many different types of thought with which mysticism may be allied:

The fact is that the mystical feeling of enlargement, union, and emancipation has no specific intellectual content whatever of its own. It is capable of forming matrimonial alliances with material furnished by the most diverse philosophies and theologies, provided only they can find a place in their framework for its peculiar emotional mood. We have no right, therefore, to invoke its prestige as distinctively in favor of any special belief, such as that in absolute idealism, or in the absolute monistic identity, or in the absolute goodness, of the world.[3]

[1] F. H. Bradley, *Appearance and Reality* (Oxford, 1930), pp. 5-6.

[2] Samuel Alexander, "Spinoza and Time," *Philosophical and Literary Pieces* (London, 1939), pp. 377-78.

[3] William James, *The Varieties of Religious Experience* (New York, 1902), pp. 416-17.

A brief consideration—necessarily sketchy and incomplete—of some of these various philosophical orientations according to which the mystical experience may be interpreted, is now in order. Like any other universal and intrinsic quality of the human psyche, its efflorescence in human life has been delineated in terms of the most general concepts linking human values to the universe—systems of philosophy and metaphysics. We wish to present very briefly some of the major philosophical implications which form the undergirding for a validation of mysticism. There are several of these systems of thought, as William James indicated. A point of departure for their examination may be suggested by Irwin Edman's quotation from St. John of the Cross: "God (contains) all creatures in himself, virtually, presentially and substantially." [4] Professor Edman then makes the significant addition crucial for our present purpose:

Substitute "Being" for "God," as many of the most religious mystics and theologians are content enough to do, and there appears a philosophical meaning that is often enough half obscured because embedded in a conventionalized theological vocabulary.[5]

The mystic's ecstasy is claimed to be a contact, a communication, indeed, a union with Being which yields such a richness, such a glory in the soul that the mystic declares it to be ineffable, inexpressible. But having said this, the mystic has usually been very voluble about what may be called the pattern of Being in which he found himself engulfed, and this cosmic, this eternal, pattern is inevitably conditioned by the theological, philosophical, and cultural orientation of the religious tradition in which he was born. At its most elementary level, this pattern of Being has been directly intuited as a changeless, timeless Unity which defies description. Here the Hindu's exclamation, "Not this, not that!" is peculiarly relevant. Or else, in its most elaborate form,

---

[4] *St. John of the Cross,* tr. E. Allison Peers, III, 210, quoted by Irwin Edman.

[5] Irwin Edman, *Four Ways of Philosophy* (New York, 1937), p. 179.

this pattern of Being has been delineated in terms of a complex theology defended by an ecclesiastical structure within which the mystical experience is constricted for good or ill.

It is possible, then, to provide a large variety of expressions of the pattern of Being, starting with its simple, unresolved unity in which all things are dissolved, to its complicated articulated form in Christian theism. Between these extremes, a number of philosophical positions may be found, such as Idealism, Naturalism, Creative and Emergent Evolution, Existentialism, and perhaps others, and all of them imply to some degree a pattern of Being which may be intuited in the mystical experience. There is nothing very strange about this since the pattern of Being which animates all things and maintains them in total relatedness also animates the individual mystic in the personal pattern of his life, and gives him the feeling, if not the conceptual statement, that he participates in this infinite, inexhaustible pattern of which he is an infinitesimal part.

Beginning our survey with the point of view which has the least implication of old-fashioned metaphysics, we find this to be the logical philosophy of L. Wittgenstein, so ably presented by Professor John A. Irving. A cardinal expression of Wittgenstein already quoted (p. 111) is: "Not *how* the world is, is the mystical, but *that* it is." *That* there is a world which defies representation, which defies expression in terms of logical symbolism, is an assertion which lies beyond the boundaries of any logical system for Wittgenstein. The contemplation of this world is therefore inexpressible, it is ineffable in the time-honored cry of the mystics, though we miss in Wittgenstein the sense of warmth, exaltation, ecstasy which are the familiar accompaniments of the experience of union with the pattern of Being. But, as the most modest of mystics, Wittgenstein would no doubt reply that he cannot express the inexpressible. Not *how* Reality is, but *that* it is, is his final consideration. He refuses to express the "thatness" of Being in terms of any pattern or structure, but his contribution is nevertheless extremely valuable in its awareness of an objective world which defies description in discursive knowledge but which elicits from him the sense of the mystical. It would seem that Wittgenstein cannot be condemned as a philosopher utterly rejecting metaphysics.[6]

Another positivist who lends some weight to the quest of the human mind for a cosmic unity is Moritz Schlick: "Our craving for knowledge . . . urgently demands a continually increasing unification of nature." [7]

The unification of the energies of nature under a universal law reconciling the forces of gravitation and electromagnetism was a lifelong task of Einstein, and it is not at all surprising that he felt the impact of the mystical vision in his tireless efforts to discover the mathematical equations for the overarching unity of the space-time universe, the mystery of that "something far more deeply interfused" than our present knowledge of universal laws affords.

Our summary of the philosophical implications of mysticism in the present chapter began with the distinct recognition by logical positivists that there is a world inexpressible in logical propositions, and that the human mind is nevertheless striving to ascertain the principle of unity of that world. Up to this point in our argument there is lacking that sense of rapturous union with the totality of things which is the familiar note to be discerned in all mystics. One could not expect a positivist with his rigorous methodology to be an ecstatic mystic! There is, however, one

[6] Whether the Vienna Circle implies a rejection of all metaphysics—whether of God, mind, or matter—is a moot point beyond the scope of this discussion. We shall content ourselves with a corrective statement by Professor Victor Kraft: "It is a complete misunderstanding of the doctrine defended by the Vienna Circle that all propositions, including those about reality, must be testable and confirmable by experience, to take it to assert that only sense-data are real, that physical objects are nothing but auxiliary constructs for ordering sense-data, that the external world is nothing but a 'logical construction' in a sense in which this implies its unreality." Victor Kraft, *The Vienna Circle* (New York, 1953), p. 178. For further discussions of Wittgenstein, see J. O. Urmson, *Philosophical Analysis* (Oxford, 1956), pp. 99-111; John Passmore, *A Hundred Years of Philosophy* (New York, 1957), pp. 352-66. Wittgenstein's approach to mysticism is also referred to by Canon Charles E. Raven in *Natural Religion and Christian Theology* (Cambridge, 1953), p. 43.

[7] Moritz Schlick, *Philosophy of Nature* (New York, 1949), p. 111.

science which lends itself to the mystical experience more than any other and this is astronomy.

The Mysticism of Science and Nature

It is a commonplace observation that modern science has given us a much more exalted idea of the almost incomprehensible reaches of the cosmos than was available even a generation ago. The mystical mood in the contemplation of the universe from which all things and all persons have evolved is bound to be interpreted, after the experience is had, in terms of the vastness of the cosmos, both in its infinitely large and in its infinitely minute aspects. It is this cosmos that the nature mystic has experienced in however involuntary and incomplete a fashion. The atom, in spite of its ultramicroscopic size, is still vast in comparison with its subatomic particles! The atom and the galaxy seem to be related through complicated mathematical formulas, so that it is not at all unusual for astronomers to feel that these equations give them what Whitehead would call a "positive prehension" of the nature and evolution of billions of stars.

These discoveries may induce in us a feeling of insignificance, of utter powerlessness over this tremendous display of cosmic forces, of obliteration when faced with magnitudes beyond our comprehension. And yet this depressing sense may give way to an appreciation of the outreach of the human mind in penetrating the cosmic depths and in revealing the astounding facts which comprise the science of astronomy. Camille Flammarion was par excellence the man who delighted the whole of Europe with his imaginative presentation of the discoveries of his beloved science —the Being of astronomy and its cosmic pattern—a cosmic pattern, by the way, far better known to Shapley than it could possibly have been to Flammarion. No one ever painted the poetry of the heavens in richer colors, in more extravagant language. For instance, he is lost in ecstasy as he computes the heating power of the sun:

It is not impossible to express this marvelous power, but we can admit without shame that it is impossible to comprehend it. The heat emitted by the sun in each second is equal to that which would result from the combustion of eleven quadrillions six hundred thousand milliards of tons of coal burning at the same time.

This same heat *would boil* per hour *seven hundred thousand mil-lions of cubic miles of water at the temperature of ice.* Attempt to understand it! As well might the ant attempt to drink the ocean! [8]

The impression of this stupendous power of the sun is so vivid that it glows with peculiar intensity as he attempts to multiply metaphors to indicate the apprehension of a cosmic fact which is beyond the power of his imagination. It gives him the feeling of what Kant called the mathematically sublime:

O popes of the Aryans! O priests of the Incas! O therapeutists of Egypt! and you philosophers of Greece, alchemists of the Middle Ages, scientists of modern times! O thinkers of all ages! You should be dumb before the sublime star! What is our voice in nature? We may pile up metaphors on metaphors, we shall only lower these magnitudes to our own size. We are but Pygmies pretending to scale the sky.[9]

In fact, the French edition contains a passage which was sup-pressed in the English translation, probably for fear of offending our Puritan religious consciousness:

Let Moses prostrate himself! Let Joshua no longer imagine that he can transmit divine orders to the sun! Let David and Isaiah no longer sing! [10]

Flammarion did not hesitate to suggest that the great figures of the Old Testament be silent in the presence of this testament of the heavens! The grandeur and sublimity of the cosmos had a most elevating effect on his soul, and he never tired of filling his many volumes with its poetry. No scientist has ever succeeded in depicting the mysticism of science with such a degree of emotional frenzy as did Flammarion. For it is especially in astronomy that we find the mysticism which is inspired by science. Flammarion was indeed a mystic of the muse of astronomy. He sang her un-

[8] Camille Flammarion, *Popular Astronomy* (New York, 1907), p. 247.
[9] *Ibid.*, p. 247.
[10] Flammarion, *Astronomie populaire* (Paris, 1922), p. 314. My translation.

surpassable glories which he appreciated to such a degree that he
had little interest in the economic and international tensions of
his own time. His Olympian disregard of the social and political
issues of his day for the sake of his own scientific vision may have
been one of his shortcomings. The only utopia that he could
conscientiously strive for was a society of men and women freed
from the scourge of war and provided with binoculars in a devotion to astronomical contemplation, so that they would be able to
exclaim:

> I saw and heard, and knew at last
> The How and Why of all things, past,
> And present, and forevermore.
> The universe, cleft to the core,
> Lay open to my probing sense.[11]

Such is the mysticism of science. It is not, of course, the only
type of mysticism, but one whose appeal cannot be denied to
those interested in the theoretical aspects of science informed by
universal laws penetrating the cosmic depths. The tone of exaltation is unmistakable. The vivid impression of a sublime experience is presented in figurative language which obviously fails
to do justice to the experience itself. Moreover, the experience is
not merely subjective. It is not simply an intellectual turmoil
with no relation to reality. To Flammarion astronomical reality
did really possess this sublime aspect, and this reality he apparently captured in a consummatory experience bringing to a
focal point the feeling of the universality and pervasiveness of
gigantic cosmic forces. He would have agreed enthusiastically
with the beautiful passage of the mystical English poet Thomas
Traherne, to be found in his *Centuries of Meditation:* "You will
never enjoy the world aright, till the Sea itself floweth in your
veins, till you are clothed with the heavens and crowned with the
stars."

Such is the mysticism of nature to which astronomy makes its
important contribution. To some the revelations of this science
displaying myriads of galaxies will be simply more of the same

[11] From *Renascence and Other Poems* (New York, 1912, 1940), copyright
by Edna St. Vincent Millay.

thing—a dull procession of galaxies without end; to others they will carry that sense of inexhaustibility which culminates in the restlessness of the human spirit when it attempts to grapple with a reality immeasurably greater than itself. The pattern of Being of Nature has indeed received new meaning through astronomy.

The Danger of an Occult Mysticism

It would not be well to leave the mysticism of science without entering a warning against current tendencies which attempt to bring scientific discoveries to the support of fantastic doctrines. There is a type of mind which cannot distinguish between astronomy and astrology, between the rigorous research of the one and the superstition of the other. In particular, atomic and nuclear theories presenting the atom as a minute center of world-shattering forces have given fresh impetus to those who wish to build strange systems of metaphysics by giving to the word "vibration" all sorts of spiritual connotations. It is true that the study of atomic energy provides a fascinating appreciation of the power and beauty of mathematical analysis. C. A. Coulson in a recent issue of *The Listener* testifies to the beauty of mathematical physics:

> I recall a series of lectures at Cambridge on wave mechanics. They were a set of lectures for the mathematical Tripos, but as they proceeded, and as one by one I saw more and more phenomena in the world of physics fitting into one great scheme—first, the energies of atoms; then their colours; then their collisions with each other; then the way they interact with X-rays, and the way they join together to form a piece of metal—I became more and more thrilled, and would gladly miss my breakfast, as indeed did occur, provided that I did not miss the next lecture of the series. This was an emotional experience akin to that in Thomas Hardy's *Dynasts* when "the Spirit of the Years opens the nether sky, and the whole of Europe is disclosed as one heaving pulsating whole, with the Alps, a backbone, and the peninsular plateau of Spain a head, and when the whole anatomy of life and movement in all humanity is exhibited as the life of one single organism." [12]

[12] C. A. Coulson, "Mathematics and Beauty," *The Listener,* XLIII (May 4, 1950), 785.

This emotional experience has a Platonic and Pythagorean touch in depicting the harmony of atomic phenomena, but there is no connection whatever between this sheer intellectual delight in mathematics and the esoteric beliefs of any "Pythagorean brotherhoods," ancient or modern. The word "nuclear" may be invested with vague spiritual meanings, but if this is done it is a wholly unscientific procedure. The energies of the atom are not spiritual energies. They are indeed fascinating to the scientific mind but in no sense to be equated with fantastic religious or mystical meanings. There is no "soul" within the atom; the forces of attraction are not to be interpreted in terms of "love," nor the forces of repulsion in terms of "hate." The rejection of a spurious "atomic" spirituality by the learned Dean of St. Paul's is significant:

> I have not been able to follow those who hold that the decomposition of material particles, which were formerly supposed to be solid and indestructible, is a valid argument in favour of a spiritual as opposed to a materialistic view of ultimate reality. Although I hold that ultimate reality is "spiritual," not material, I cannot admit that matter dissolved into radiation is more "spiritual" than matter in a solid or liquid state. We may refuse to call it any longer matter, but this is not a refutation of materialism. This argument, which is used by some Christian apologists, seems to me frivolous.[13]

It is necessary to emphasize this point, for frantic attempts are sometimes made to interpret atomic vibrations, nuclear reactions, cosmic rays in a spiritual and pseudomystical sense. And

[13] William Ralph Inge, *God and the Astronomers* (New York, 1933), p. viii. The materialist who has a sense of ecstasy at the glory of qualities supported by matter is closer to mysticism than the occultist who generally requires a much more formidable array of supernatural paraphernalia to account for his experiences. I shall always remember the joy which suffused the face of Professor Donald Williams when he made the following statement to his class in metaphysics at Harvard in 1950: "The glory of existence is the rich concreteness of things, the unimaginable diversity of things. The richness and quality of a pinhead is beyond description. According to most philosophers, it has something greater than any combination of qualities, it has the miracle and glory and grace of existence. Existence per se is a kind of glory." For a discussion of occult mysticism see also Paul Tillich, *The Religious Situation* (New York, 1956), pp. 166-71.

yet no physicist of note gives any warrant for such unscientific extrapolations. In the words of Lawrence P. Lessing,

> Cosmic rays . . . have no relation to astrology, cosmogony, or any of the other dubious arts . . . other romancers try to incorporate cosmic rays into mystical systems on a par with Rosicrucianism, as emanations from the universal soul.[14]

A further objection may be raised to such fantastic theories. They represent an infringement of man's dignity and freedom. According to these strange doctrines, spiritual energy in its purest essence is presumed to be found within the atom, and the mind of man is merely a conglomeration, even a degradation, of this energy which can be overcome only by placing the mind "in tune" with these mysterious vibrations, and thereby enjoying thrills believed to produce quite tangible material and emotional benefits in this world and the next! In this type of occult mysticism with its accent on atomic vibrations and "radiations" there is a distinct materialistic flavor which is repellent to all who find the richness and beauty of the spiritual life not in extremely minute atomic phenomena, but on a much higher level, in the mind and soul of man. The human spirit possesses inalienable freedom to evaluate alternatives, to make moral judgments, to respond to its own categorical imperatives of duty and service, and eventually to control atomic discoveries and processes for human welfare. What Wordsworth calls "man's unconquerable mind" is stated by Dean Willard L. Sperry to be—

> the most impressive thing we know here and now. We follow its gradual emergence from its animal beginnings, we trace its tremendous acceleration since the dawn of civilization, we record its almost incredible achievements in the last hurrying century of science.[15]

Surely such a mind is not to be dragged down to subservience to mysterious "mystical" atomic vibrations at the dictates of esoteric Theosophists even when they appear in the guise of investigators of comparative religion and pretend to give us the benefits of

[14] Lawrence P. Lessing, *Fortune Magazine* (February, 1949), pp. 110, 144.
[15] Willard L. Sperry, *What We Mean by Religion* (New York, 1940), p. 146.

Oriental wisdom. There is no evidence whatsoever to indicate that any of the great spirits of our time who incarnate the mind of the East—such as Gandhi, Nehru, Tagore, for instance—have ever given any support to the astrological lore which forms a large part of Theosophy. The sober judgment of James Bissett Pratt, a religious thinker sympathetic to mysticism, is significant.[16]

No, it is not by imagining that intra-atomic forces and vibrations are electrical and assumed to be nonmaterial that we can jump to the conclusion that the nonmaterial is to be automatically equated with the spiritual. Nor is the view of Jeans and Eddington that atoms are thoughts in the mind of God accepted at all widely by their fellows in the sciences of physics and astronomy. I do not wish to labor the point, but it is pertinent to observe that no thinking person, no serious student of religion, will have the slightest regard for mysticism if this experience is to be understood in terms of the fantastic and the esoteric. We may well be guided by Dean Inge's significant and forthright statement:

> Necromancy, astrology, alchemy, palmistry, and spiritualism are the reproach of mysticism, and have nothing to do with the philosophy which is our subject.[17]

---

[16] See James B. Pratt, *India and Its Faith* (Boston, 1915), chapter XI, "The Radhasoamis and Theosophists," pp. 213-34. The following is taken from pp. 233-34: "For in spite of the unmistakable good that the Theosophical Society has done in India its influence has had two results that are quite as unmistakably evil. In the first place, at this time when India is just awakening to modern thought and is in such need of careful guidance, Theosophy has not only encouraged most of its old superstitions, but has taught it to identify science with obscurantism and occultism and to found the new structure of its faith on those very shifting sands. And what is perhaps more dangerous still, in its blind effort to attack 'materialism' it has brought the spirit into contempt and derision by spreading abroad the view that 'spirituality' means a belief in psychic planes, vibrations, magnetism, and mantras. Surely not thus shall we triumph over 'materialism.' Surely not such is the message that shall set the spirit free."

From conversations with Professor N. A. Nikam while Visiting Fellow at Yale University in 1952-53 I was happy to learn that the mysticism of the Upanishads has little to do with Theosophy.

[17] Inge, *Mysticism in Religion,* pp. 164-65.

The Mysticism of the Timeless

The type of mysticism which has had a distinguished history in the Western religious tradition, and which has some affinity with the mysticism of the East, is that associated with Platonism and Neoplatonism. Sometimes it is allied with philosophic Idealism, and whether Platonic realism is rightly subsumed under the category of Idealism is an issue which we shall leave to the professional philosophers. It is true that this tradition of Platonism and Idealism in philosophy has been to a large degree displaced in the last fifty years by vigorous evolutionism and realism, but it is also the case that these later developments have not as yet realized their potentiality as philosophic supports of a modern mysticism.

The mysticism of the Timeless, of Eternal Values, however, still has distinguished representatives, such as W. R. Inge. He emphasizes its relation to the structure of Reality, that structure which we have called the pattern of Being. For him the vision of the mystic has some objective reference:

> Some, I suppose, would say that the question of the objectivity of the vision falls outside the scope of philosophy also, since in their opinion all truth is relative, and the quest of the absolute is vain. But those who believe this must remain forever outside the world in which the mystic moves. For mysticism is essentially ontological; the contemplative cares nothing for states of consciousness. His business is with the ultimately real. He aspires to the vision of God, and believes that this vision is within his reach.[18]

In such a philosophy the vision of the Real is best interpreted as the apprehension of the absolute values of Truth, Goodness, and Beauty, which are held to be revelations of God. These are eternal values dwelling not primarily in this world of change, struggle, frustration, misery, and tragedy, but rather in the mysterious realm of the Eternal, "beyond this bourne of time and

---

[18] *Ibid.,* p. 152. Dean Inge's emphasis on ontology rather than psychology in his study of mysticism is well worth stressing: "I have given my reasons for refusing to treat mysticism in religion as a branch of psychology or of psychopathology. Mysticism deals not with states of consciousness, but with ultimate reality, or it is nothing." *Ibid.,* p. 55.

place." Dean Inge is at pains to show that in no sense can we interpret Eternity as simply the unending passage of time. It is a category in itself, the ultimately real category in fact, so that our world of everyday experience pales into insignificance beside it— not exactly the insignificance of oblivion, but rather that of being a shadow world. It is a true shadow, but its radiant original lies beyond our present temporal existence unless perchance the mystical vision affords us a glimpse of its gleaming towers.

This derogation of the universe of space-time indicates why the learned Dean was never perturbed by the second law of thermo-dynamics which he fervently believed meant the death of the universe in random motion. Space-time or no space-time, Dean Inge held on to eternal values, confident they did not have their abiding place in any spatial or temporal regions.

The characteristic meaning of this type of mysticism is, then, derived from the contemplation of an order of Reality assumed to exist beyond the exigencies of our temporal existence. In the vision of Eternity the awareness of "before" and "after" disap-pears in an "eternal now," a *nunc stans,* in which all our strivings, all our aspirations, all our uncertainties, all our anxieties are resolved into that inward peace gained through the vision of the Immutable One in which all partial truths, all divisions, all con-flicts are immobilized into a divine unity. The efforts of our daily life involved in the ceaseless passing of time are perceived to be contaminated with a degree of illusion, since time is metaphysi-cally—that is to say, in the deepest perception of the ultimate nature of things—unreal. This mysticism obviously stresses the unreality of time and the unreality of our everyday world for the sake of the infinitely greater reality of that ineffable Eternal World existing in a timeless, immutable perfection.

No doubt when meeting with disaster and despair, with hope deferred or extinguished, we tend to that yearning for ultimate release from the trials of our existence, for that escape which Plotinus called "the flight of the alone to the Alone." But do we not sense a danger that we may turn our backs upon our respon-sibilities, however imperious they may be, and retire into the contemplation of that Reality which is said to be above all tribulations? Is there not a danger that we may relinquish our earthly duties, especially when these are harassing, that we may persuade ourselves that this world is merely the shadow world of unreality? The danger is real. It is exemplified by the *via negativa*—a way of mysticism rejected by the best exemplars—in the renunciation not merely of the evil things of this world, but of the good things as well, for the vision of the completely Other. It may be the source of those frenzied quests for experience vouchsafed to a so-called spiritual elite, but which reflect all too often the marks of the pathological. The late Douglas Clyde Macintosh, a distinguished theologian not averse to a sane mysticism, nevertheless admitted:

> It is a well-recognized fact that the mystic's experience often includes an element of hallucination, frequently recognized as such by the mystic himself. The records of mystical experience abound with accounts of special visions, auditions, feelings of motion, and the like. Sometimes, at least from our point of view, the experience has been unmistakably hallucinatory, as when Plotinus saw the celestial Venus, or when the Holy Babe "appeared" to Suso and to Ignatius Loyola hundreds of years after he had ceased to be a babe in arms.[19]

This is not to say that the mysticism proffered by philosophical Idealists and Platonists necessarily culminates in such a formless, escapist, or hallucinatory experience. When the mysticism of the timeless is centered on the vision of truth, goodness and beauty as impregnated, however imperfectly, in our everyday life and in our fellow human beings, extreme forms of escape are held in check. When, however, the timeless element in such mysticism predominates, when the world of our experience is held to be illusion, mere appearance, a mere shadow of the real world beyond time and space, is there not a tendency for that type of otherworldly mysticism to be in fact a flight to the world of the timeless, the immutable, the eternal?

A significant aspect of this mystical conception, so strange to our Western world filled with activity, striving, and effort, is that against the background of the unreality of time, our goals, pur-

[19] Douglas Clyde Macintosh, *The Problem of Religious Knowledge* (New York, 1940), p. 33.

poses, and values seem to lose their meaning. Under the vision of an "eternal now" there is no longer any distinction of "before" and "after," and those vexing problems which demand our atten-tion and even our self-sacrifice, those commitments which require a reaffirmation of our democratic values, those world conditions which at times necessitate excruciating efforts—all these belong to the world of "appearance." In the world of eternity, all these problems, efforts, strivings have been completed to the last degree of temporal existence, since the whole of temporal existence is included within the eternal and the timeless. In other words, the whole earthly drama, the total historical flow of our existence with its sufferings and tragedies in the world of time is in reality already consummated; it is already terminated down to the last iota in the world of the eternal! We are merely fighting shadow battles in a shadow world! Even those who sympathize with the mysticism of God as the timeless Absolute realize its unsolved problems:

> How shall it heal my hurt now to know that "in the long run" or "on the whole" my evil is God's good or the good of the whole universe? . . . If I choose wrong, I know that my failure will some-how, *sub specie aeternitatis*, redound to the glory of the Absolute; if I do right, my contribution is only that of the fly to the moving wheel.[20]

The strictures of William James in his *Pragmatism* are too well known to bear repetition here.[21] Nevertheless, the reader who

---

[20] Charles A. Bennett, *A Philosophical Study of Mysticism* (New Haven, 1923), pp. 89, 120. Another criticism of absolutism is the following: "Re-ligiously, absolutism is defective. While absolutism seems to be harmonious with the mystical sense of oneness with God (the *unio mystica*), it imperils other sides of religion. If the soul is literally one with God in its very being, then man's responsibility and his moral life as a person are at an end. Only God is responsible for God. To cancel moral endeavor is to cut the root of prophetic religion everywhere and to destroy the tie between religion and human character." Edgar Sheffield Brightman, *Person and Reality,* ed. Peter Anthony Bertocci (New York, 1958), p. 299.

[21] A stricture which will bear repetition, however, is the following: "An idealistic religion is one that is purely spiritual; which rests on the separa-tion of the spiritual from the material, and which finds its function in the

wishes to explore more fully the mysticism of the timeless, and who feels that what has been given here is a one-sided evaluation, is encouraged to consult the following works: *Mysticism in Religion* by William Ralph Inge; *The Supreme Identity, an Essay in Oriental Metaphysics and the Christian Religion* by Alan Watts; and *Time and Eternity* by W. T. Stace. The latter volume is an able presentation of the subject by an eminent idealistic philosopher who also claims naturalistic tendencies. Also informative on Oriental philosophy and the mysticism of the East is F. S. C. Northrop's *The Meeting of East and West*. All of these authors are perfectly able to present the mysticism of the timeless in very persuasive terms relevant to the modern, Western, activist mind so puzzling to the Oriental thinker, and to point out grave shortcomings in our civilization and religion.

The Mysticism of the Creativeness of All Reality

Since mysticism has, in the opinion of its critics, all too often attached itself to escapist visions and pathological experiences, there are those who will insist that we be done with mysticism, that it is an evil growth to be plucked out in our examination of various philosophies of religion. This is not, however, our conviction; for the deficiencies of that type of mysticism in which time is held to be unreal, as well as of the spurious kind of mysticism associated with esoteric fantasies, may be overcome once we accept the reality of time as an irreducible component of being. Once we do this our efforts, goals, ideals, acquire fresh meaning and urgency. They are the work of our hands, the fruits of our endeavors, and they derive their justification from the continuity

---

spiritual field. It is a religion which has lost its reference to this world—the material world of food and work, of business and politics and war. It is *above* material considerations. Because it is not about this world, it exists for our comfort and satisfaction. It is our refuge from the sorrows and the evils of this life, and we retire from the world to enter the realm of ideas and images which it has built for our consolation. . . . To escape from idealism religion must recover its reference to the actuality of this world, and to the immediacy of the present as the point of action in this life." John Macmurray, *Idealism against Religion* (London, 1944), pp. 17, 18.

of the life of humanity within the continuity of the larger, vaster life of a space-time universe in which values may be created, nurtured, and fulfilled. Such a view leads to a dynamic rather than to a static mysticism, and its philosophical implication and support is obviously different from that of the mysticism of the timeless. It may be found in the emphatic declaration of the reality of the world as change, as process, given by John Laird, one of the chief representatives of the philosophy of becoming:

> The theory of the creativeness of all reality denies the legitimacy of trying to find an explanation of becoming itself, that is to say, it refuses to peer behind the scenes in order to find something that makes going go. It declares that process, transition or becoming is wholly ultimate. In many expositions of Christian metaphysics the contrary is assumed. It is held that existence is ultimate while time or becoming is not. God's existence, the great "I am," is said to be ultimate. There is no sense in going behind it, no sense in asking what originated it; but anything that *begins to be* (according to this theory) must be originated. The theory of creative actuality denies this conception *in toto,* and asserts that all existence is ultimately existential becoming. Consequently there is no sense in supposing that any existent, divine or secular, non-natural or natural, originates the process of becoming.[22]

In a somewhat similar argument, Robert J. Hutcheon, a theologian of undoubted liberalism, also held to "the creativeness of all reality":

> No simile can make intelligible to us the creation of matter out of nothing. Creation is not an event in some definite time, for time is a constituent of the very substance of reality. The universe, using that term in its most inclusive sense, is not an effect of something outside itself. The totality of things is self-existing, self-moving, self-sustaining. . . . God for religion has always meant that phase or those phases of experienced reality which seemed to have most bearing on actual human values.[23]

A self-moving, self-sustaining universe in which creative advances take place, not according to a foreordained plan in God's vision of an eternal present but according to an immanent, per-

---

[22] John Laird, *Theism and Cosmogony* (London, 1940), p. 315.
[23] R. J. Hutcheon, *Frankness in Religion* (New York, 1929), pp. 136, 137.

haps tentative creativity, leads inevitably to a radically different conception of God than that found in traditional Christianity. The contrast is clear from the following quotation from Newton P. Stallknecht and Robert S. Brumbaugh:

> If there is a God responsible for the existence and growth of natural objects he does not guide their course according to an immanent and complete plan. He does not see all times and all places following from his own nature or from the nature of the universe. His providence does not exhaust the future. Rather, as Bergson has it, creation must fashion its path as it advances; and so must a creative God.[24]

The philosophic foundation for that type of mysticism in which time is real may be located in those various world views in which reality is interpreted in terms of process, of emergent evolution, of holism, of evolutionary naturalism, even of a materialism of levels as represented by Roy Wood Sellars and Marvin Farber. Well does H. N. Wieman, a naturalistic theologian who utilizes the theory of levels of reality in his thought, summarize these philosophic trends:

> It is what Smuts calls Holism, Hobhouse calls cooperation, Whitehead the principle of concretion, Pupin creative coordination, S. Alexander and Lloyd Morgan the nisus toward ever higher creative syntheses, Hocking the Whole Idea. These philosophies cannot all be lumped together as identical, of course, but there is a common strain running through them all.[25]

We shall relegate the technical discussion of these systems of emergence and their varied emphases to the philosophers who are specialists in their investigation. We are primarily interested in the pattern of being—to use our common formula—represented by these world views, a pattern called by Wieman the "process of progressive integration." He adds a word of caution:

> But we are not saying that the whole universe in every phase of its being is steadily moving toward increased integration. We are only

[24] Newton P. Stallknecht and Robert S. Brumbaugh, *The Compass of Philosophy* (New York, 1954), p. 137.

[25] Henry Nelson Wieman, *Methods of Private Religious Living* (New York, 1928), p. 52.

saying that amid all the different tendencies of the universe, this progressive integration is one.[26]

To be sure, the trend toward progressive integration does not deny the well-known second law of thermodynamics, but neither is it denied by this law. The progressive integration manifested in the universe has received attention by Roy Wood Sellars in his evolutionary naturalism as a principle of organization. Distinguished biologists such as Woodger, Bertalanffy, Sinnott, have reinforced this concept as that of the self-sustaining, self-regulating capacity of the myriads of living organisms as they evolved in time from relatively simple ancestors. They call it "the principle of organization." In his recent volume, *The Biology of the Spirit,* Edmund W. Sinnott asserts on the basis of a mass of evidence he has so ably presented:

The upward, purposeful thrust of life, which continually opposes the downward drag of matter, is evidence, I think, that in nature there is something we may call—to name what never can be put into words—a Principle of Organization. Not only does it lift man ever higher but it provides three great essentials for his religion—it brings order out of randomness, spirit out of matter, and personality out of neutral and impersonal stuff. . . . Words are feeble things to express an idea so vast, but the conception of an organizing force, something that not only holds the universe together and builds within it orderly patterns of matter, from atoms and stars and galaxies to man, but continually lifts life upward from the simple processes of protoplasm to the highest levels of man's spiritual nature, seems no unworthy expression of such an ineffable quality as God's nature must possess.[27]

[26] *Ibid.,* p. 53.

[27] Edmund W. Sinnott, *The Biology of the Spirit* (New York, 1955), pp. 161, 162-63. See also *Matter, Mind and Man, World Perspectives, Vol. 11* (New York, 1957). The availability of a philosophy of emergent forms for the interpretation of mysticism may also be found in Lancelot Law Whyte, *Accent on Form, World Perspectives* (New York, 1954), II, 190-91: "The affirmation must be of a principle pervading all nature and known to each of us in our own nature, which enables us to face distress and destruction. It should be so general and so deep that we are not shaken by any particular disaster. . . . The supreme beauty has to be recognized in the general forming power, rather than in any particular form. If that recognition could be achieved and sustained, nothing would shake us."

Fully consonant with this expression of the Principle of Organization is the philosophy of Samuel Alexander in which is deployed the evolution of space-time characterized by the emergence of higher syntheses as complications of this fundamental space-time matrix. The mind of man is the highest synthesis of space-time, though Alexander in a daring mood extended this evolution to beings higher than man, his favorite finite gods, and ultimately to Deity. More germane for our discussion is his conception of the nisus: "There is a nisus in Space-Time which, as it has borne its creatures forward through matter and life to mind, will bear them forward to some higher level of existence." [28]

This abstract conception is nevertheless related to our religious sense, even to the communion and passion involved in religion:

> Sharing in the nisus of the universe; caught as we are in the wheels of that being . . . we respond to that nisus in the feeling of oneness with the next higher type of quality which is to arise out of the level we or other minds have attained. . . . Because the whole world in its nisus to deity evokes in us the response of religion, we become aware of the world as in this tendency divine, and apprehend God, as we apprehend the object of love to be lovely. The religious passion which we find in ourselves cries out for an object which intellect then sets itself the task of describing in intellectual terms, discovering its relation to observed realities.[29]

It is to be noted that this philosophic language is not far removed from the familiar affirmations of the mystic. We share in the nisus of the universe and respond to it in the feeling of oneness with the divine qualities which this nisus or organizing

---

[28] Samuel Alexander, *Space, Time, and Deity,* The Gifford Lectures at Glasgow, 1916-18 (New York, 1950), II, 346. Lack of space prevents discussion of a work somewhat similar to that of Alexander. This is Charles Francis Potter's *Creative Personality* (New York, 1950). The cosmic orientation of Dr. Potter's humanism represents a trend in the religious humanist movement which is favorable to evolutionary philosophy. Another trend in humanism is satisfied to comprehend mysticism as a relation to a "vital principle of betterment" where the cosmic orientation is not explicitly formulated. Such a mysticism is represented in this symposium by the essays of Kenneth Patton and J. Hutton Hynd.

[29] Alexander, "Spinoza and Time," *Philosophical and Literary Pieces,* pp. 383-84.

emergent power brings forth in time. We are caught in the creative pattern of this emergent process, and this involvement of our
lives with the nisus of space-time is not merely the apprehension
of an abstract philosophical conception. This involvement is
manifested emotionally as nothing less than the highest religious
passion. Alexander was profoundly aware of the necessity of mysticism in religion:

> There is a sound and a dangerous mysticism. The sound variety is
> an essential ingredient in all religion; it is not too much to say that
> it is the vital ingredient of religion, without which religion is a
> thing of forms.[30]

Alexander, however, was not the only philosopher of Becoming
to stress the relevance of his ontology to religion and to mysticism.
Bergson in his *Two Sources of Morality and Religion* developed
further his conception of the *élan vital* elaborated in *Creative
Evolution* and related it directly to the mystical experience. This
is not the place to summarize this important work but it is significant for our present purpose to realize that Bergson described
mysticism as "an effort at oneness with the creative impetus." [31]
After a lucid discussion in which he did full justice to the mystical experience as the ecstasy of union with a God of love, he
interpreted this experience in terms of his conception of a universe of life arising from depths of material substance:

> There is nothing to prevent the philosopher from following to its
> logical conclusion the idea which mysticism suggests to him of a
> universe which is the mere visible and tangible aspect of love and
> of the need of loving, together with all the consequences entailed
> by this creative emotion: I mean the appearance of living creatures
> in which this emotion finds its complement; of an infinity of other
> beings without which they could not have appeared, and lastly of
> the unfathomable depths of material substance without which life
> would not have been possible.[32]

[30] *Ibid.*, p. 377.

[31] Henri Bergson, *The Two Sources of Morality and Religion* (New York,
1935), p. 214.

[32] *Ibid.*, p. 244. A mystical interpretation based on Bergson's evolutionary
views will not be appreciated by most Christian philosophers. For instance,
such a liberal thinker as Theodore Meyer Greene all too easily dismisses two

Man is, then, a cosmic culmination of the vital impulse, of the creative, integrative forces of the universe symbolized as God— a culmination resting dynamically on a number of levels of living forms manifesting lower degrees of organization, themselves resting on "unfathomable depths of material substance." All these levels of integration and of organization are present in man so that he is in a very real sense a concretion, a synthesis, a "whole" of the creativity of the universe. And when this creativity is conceived no longer as a static, immutable power completely transcending the universe—the "Wholly Other" of neo-orthodox theologians—but as immanent within the dynamic Principle of Organization manifested in all life, then it is reasonable to suggest that in terms of the philosophy of Becoming, the mystical experience is nothing less than the sense of ineffable union with this creative principle which sustains man's life and highest values,

---

major philosophers of our own time: "Bergson draws only to a limited degree upon the central insights of the Hebraic-Christian tradition, and Whitehead hardly at all." *Our Cultural Heritage* (Houston, 1956), p. 102. Compare the much more sympathetic approach of His Highness Sri Jaya Chamarajendra Wadiyar Bahadur in *Dattatreya, The Way and the Goal* (London, 1957), p. 14: "Bergson . . . applies his philosophy of creative evolution to religion . . . and finds in mystic experience at its best, nature's way of rising to a higher level of life." Also, p. 15: "Mystic experience therefore becomes a way of expressing the direction and meaning of evolution and so receives support from nature and science." This impasse between Indian philosophers who appreciate Western evolutionary philosophy, and Christian theologians who do not, as a basis for mysticism may perhaps be resolved by directly challenging the usual dualistic interpretation of mystical experience, such as that of Evelyn Underhill. This has been done by Canon Charles E. Raven in his Gifford Lectures expressing his profound appreciation of emergent philosophies, *Experience and Interpretation* (Cambridge, 1953), pp. 206-07: "It will be evident that the treatment of mysticism here briefly stated differs widely from that in Evelyn Underhill's great book on the subject. . . . We debated in a long series of letters the fundamental issue of her dualism. . . . It seemed to me then, and it seems still, that on her premises she was bound in the last resort to identify the mystic way with negation and to accept so sharp a cleavage between natural and supernatural as to endanger any fully incarnational philosophy. . . . It seems clear that a fresh survey of the whole subject in the light of a less Cartesian background and of recent psychological researches would be timely."

indeed suffuses his life so completely that he no longer knows whether he is conscious of the universe or whether the universe has become conscious in him! The symbolic language of the mystic involving such material imagery as "fierce glow," "vital heat," "flame," "illumination," "irradiation," "enlightenment," "light," etc., seems to be much more in agreement with the conception of the divine as emergent creativity rather than with the more traditional idea of a timeless absolute.

Is this mysticism based on evolutionary doctrines far removed from the mysticism of the East, with its culmination in the union of atman and Brahman? Not necessarily, for according to the interpretation given by Radhakrishnan:

> There is a perfect correspondence between the inner nature of man (atman) and the truth of external reality (Brahman). Man is a microcosm who participates in all strata of the universe, mineral, plant, animal, human and spiritual. All forces are potentially present in him and the universe continues the creative process through him. He has now to shape his world and himself, according to the creative powers he has.[33]

It is clear from the evidence offered by these philosophers of evolution that mysticism may be freed from the immobilizing influence which is often associated with the vision of a timeless world. Under the conception of the creativeness of all reality, the significant and outstanding religious personality is one with the creative struggle for the enlargement of human life, one with the cosmic process of integration which animates the organization of all life, one with the very pattern of being as *élan vital* or as principle of organization. The mysticism which may be ours may then begin with the appreciation of our part in this creative process, of our gratitude in being sustained by it, and of our dignity in adding our own limited contribution to its ongoing march to ever more comprehensive "wholes" of organization, to fuller expansion of the spiritual potentialities of the human spirit.

The remembrance of mystical experience at its peak might per-

[33] Sarvepalli Radhakrishnan, *Recovery of Faith, World Perspectives* (New York, 1955), IV, 148.

haps be interpreted according to one definition of poetry as "emotion recollected in tranquillity." But this would be a hard-won tranquillity, the resting place before our fresh immersion in the struggle, the emotion in which we call to mind all that has been won for us by heroic souls of the past. This resting place is merely the "withdrawal" before the "return" to our duties and responsibilities with new vigor and enthusiasm. It can never be a complete withdrawal, but is merely the prelude to our resumption of our part in that "creative cosmic struggle" of which Wieman speaks. To share in this struggle, Wieman calls for discipline, energy, calmness of spirit, mastery, health, sensitivity, and finally—

> a mystic method for achieving insight in the midst of the most complex and baffling problems of life. All this religious men and women must have if they are to be the shock troops of the integrating process of the universe. And all this they can have. All this in some measure the great religious personalities of history have had.[34]

Before we leave our brief discussion of emergent philosophy, there is one type which is peculiarly relevant to the mystical experience as a synoptic vision of the whole, and which deserves special mention. This is the "holism" of Jan Christian Smuts, distinguished statesman and philosopher. According to his work, *Holism and Evolution,* emergence is not merely the addition of a new and higher quality to a complex material organization, but is based on a more fundamental characteristic. This is—

> the character of the wholeness, the tendency to wholes, ever more intensive and effective wholes, which is basic to the universe, and of which emergence or creativeness is but one feature, however important it is in other respects.[35]

Smuts's philosophy is relevant to religious mysticism in two ways. Firstly, the ever more intensive and effective wholes are nothing less than the supremely significant religious personalities to be considered presently. Secondly, the wholes formed by the universe—atom, molecule, cell, the marvelously unified and inte-

[34] Henry Nelson Wieman, *Methods of Private Religious Living,* p. 217.
[35] Jan Christian Smuts, *Holism and Evolution* (New York, 1926), p. 321.

grated organization of all organisms, simple and complex—are apprehended by that intuitive reason which grasps their togetherness as "wholes" without being able to state precisely in what way the parts are united in the whole. This is, of course, not a denial of the task of scientific investigation and of discursive reason in discovering the relations of the parts to each other and their function in the whole. The man of science would be the first to admit that this task is inexhaustible, but before it is ever completed, we do possess this distinct awareness of a whole of qualities. It is important to note, however, that the intuitive reason which perceives a whole of qualities, such as Tennyson's flower in the crannied wall, is related to the mystical intuition which is precisely the "total-working" of the mind. Such operation is described by Charles A. Bennett:

> In it the mind apprehends the whole. It is synoptic. It is intuitive, not analytic; noetic, not discursive. It is not a process of attaching predicates to a subject but it is a knowledge of the subject of predicates.[36]

A philosophy which stresses the creative work of the universe as the formation of wholes, and a description of mystical intuition as the apprehension of these wholes, would seem to be singularly well suited to illustrate our fundamental assumption: mysticism as the experience of the pattern of being of the universe, an experience of surpassing richness and ineffability.

This pattern of being we have discussed as dimly and inarticulately apprehended by Wittgenstein as the "thatness" of reality which cannot be expressed in logical propositions. It was more adequately sung by Flammarion as the mysticism of the intellectual love of the cosmos, which is akin to Spinoza's intellectual love of God as Substance. Not merely the immensity of the cosmological facts but the sublimity of the eternal values is realized in the mysticism of the timeless. The mysticism of the creativeness of all reality, however, marked a significant departure into a new metaphysical orientation—that of becoming, emergence, holism. In each case, as we move from the logical studies of Wittgenstein

[36] Charles A. Bennett, *A Philosophical Study of Mysticism*, p. 97.

to emergent philosophies and their bearing on religion, our apprehension of the pattern of being is enriched, made more complete, more adequate to the infinite heights and depths of cosmic creativity. A final step remains to be explored, that of the emergence of the saints and prophets as more intense and effective expressions of what Smuts calls the general holistic tendency of the universe, those whom Wieman calls by militant metaphor "the shock troops of the integrating process of the universe."

Personal Mysticism

Alexander speaks of good and great men as "men of transcendent gifts of perfection" and as exemplars of the "nisus" which points to the fuller emergence of the divine in the life of the world and of human society. It is now necessary to attempt to relate more fully the dynamic mysticism just discussed to that veneration of great personalities which characterizes the world religions. It may well be that the mythologies and Christologies constructed by theologians are but the result of our human intellect and intuition being too weak and imperfect to depict the mysterious emergence of those significant personalities—the prophets and founders of religion.

What is their character? When we contemplate the lives of these religious giants we discover that they all incarnate some quality of the spiritual which brings satisfaction and even exaltation to their followers. Each religious giant, whether he be in the Jewish, Christian, Buddhist, or Hindu tradition, has a peculiar way of radiating his own spirituality, and of doing so with great intensity. We can even suggest that the "spiritual" is that mode of behavior of the human spirit in which a man lives a life of such intense quality that we no longer know whether the man lives in this quality or whether this quality lives in him. There, in so far as we can discern, is the real meaning of that highly tenuous term, "spiritual"—that intense quality of life, that close union between the quality and the man who lives it so that we can never perceive the man apart from the quality nor the quality apart from the man who exemplifies it to such a superlative degree. The quality of life and the person who lives it are completely mingled, suffused in indestructible unity. The religious giant who incarnates this quality is evidently mystically unified with it. Perhaps in this way it is possible to give a new meaning to the old symbol of the Incarnation—an integration, a culmination of mysterious cosmic forces which reach their supreme fulfillment in this intense, ideal, and harmonious quality which shines as a peak of glorious human achievement. This is the spiritual quality in man —the blazing light of the human spirit.

And this quality is not merely intensely represented in one person; it is also universal. It is universal in at least two senses. When a religious giant incarnates a quality of life, his followers feel the presence of this quality in him and respond to it in unmistakable terms. They feel its impact on their consciousness as a larger dimension of life which is beyond their own littleness, adding joy and victory to their own experience. In the second place, the spiritual is universal in the sense that the course of history, the development of new civilizations, the alterations and obliterations of cultures, do not materially affect its appeal. It is deeper than any one of these changes. We in the twentieth century still respond to the fire of divine discontent of the Hebrew prophets. Likewise, the specifically Christian ideals of good will and the redemptive power of sacrificial love have not been suppressed by their Nietzschean detractors. Similarly, the Hindu emphasis on oneness with the universe, so ably described by Professor N. A. Nikam, still elicits the aspirations, nay, the devotion of East and West. The passion for truth as expressed in scientific research may also be given the reverence due to a high spiritual quality—though, contrary to the opinion of some humanists, it is not the only spiritual quality.

Here, then, are five dimensions of the human spirit, five expressions of universal values which have appeared in history as excellences of spirituality: the demand for justice; the action of mercy and outgoing love; the achievement of self-mastery; the sense of mystical union with reality; the search for scientific truth for its own sake. It is not implied that these are the only dimensions of the human spirit, but they are among the major values found in both Eastern and Western religions and cultures. So long as these values are considered merely abstract ideals, distant visions, they do not of course possess that compelling power which produces the exaltation of mysticism. But once presented to us as vital principles in the lives of religious giants who give them radiant power, their persuasive force is inescapable. Yet these qualities do not simply flow out or radiate "on the waves of the etheric" to conquer every heart and mind. No such Pollyanna version of spirituality is here meant. On the contrary, spiritual giants, because of their very intensity and inflexible purpose, are bound to challenge "the powers of evil" of their times, and in so doing they manifest their peculiar spiritual value heroically, even when deserted by their followers. It is this heroic dimension which Whitehead has in mind when he speaks of solitariness:

> The great religious conceptions which haunt the imaginations of civilized mankind are scenes of solitariness: Prometheus chained to his rock, Mahomet brooding in the desert, the meditations of the Buddha, the solitary Man on the Cross. It belongs to the depth of the religious spirit to have felt forsaken, even by God.[37]

The deeply religious personality is not delivered from the misery and suffering of this world by magical or supernatural means. He fully endures these sufferings with his inner vision unimpaired, his idealism unabated, and his inner soul in peace and serenity. Just as a great artist is able to give the impression of artlessness and pure effortlessness, so the artist of the spiritual life, even in his moment of greatest trial, likewise radiates the force of his personality with seeming effortlessness and sheer artistry. It is this hard-won intensity mingled with peace and serenity which appears in bold relief in those solitary, heroic, and even tragic moments in the life of the religious prophet. The meaning of the age-old symbolism of light and darkness is then fully apparent. It represents the contrast between the spiritual giant exemplifying a quality destined to bring light and life to future generations and the forces of evil bringing him down to his

[37] A. N. Whitehead, *Religion in the Making*, pp. 19-20.

death. But within this contrast, the intense light of the human spirit shines ever more brightly, going forward with the deep conviction that whatever the outcome may be, this is the supreme way of life.

Through its very fidelity, however, the solitary act of the prophet does not remain in isolation—it becomes an act of communication, of communion with all humanity, haunting, in the words of Whitehead, "the imaginations of civilized mankind." The spiritual catharsis which we experience in the spectacle of a tragedy or a great heroic action gives us some conception of that sense of elevation of soul, of that mystical communion through which the devoted followers of a religious giant receive the full force of the spiritual quality incarnated in his solitary experience. This very scene of solitariness through its impact on our consciousness becomes the supreme ground of communion! It is thus that the most penetrating impressions of the religious life are received. It is thus that they are recaptured through commemorative rituals in which the original drama is re-enacted.

Borrowing some terms from the philosophy of existentialism, one might venture the opinion that the religious giant, while incarnating a quality more completely than has ever been done, cannot rely on any previous pattern but in a real sense *makes himself* in his supreme moment of dedication. And humanity at large, through the centuries, finds itself inescapably "engaged" by this glorious vision.[38]

Mystical communion with great souls at the moment of their supreme trial and victory represents the mystical dimension in its typically personal form. The fascination which we experience in attempting to come to grips with these superb lives, the straining of our spirits to grasp their essential quality of greatness, is the clearest indication—unworthy as we undoubtedly are—of our

[38] The fusion of the great religious personality with the quality of life he represents may also be interpreted in terms of the unity of being and action which is stressed by some existentialist philosophers. This meaning was suggested in John Wild's address to the Yale Philosophy Club, February 24, 1958 on "Contemporary Phenomenology and the Problem of Existence."

kinship with them, of our communion with the universal values they manifest, of our common source in the ground of reality which sustains us all.[39]

This mysticism, experienced at the human level, is essentially humanistic in tone. It may be interpreted, as did Dean Willard L. Sperry, as a humanism of—

> the social gospel, when it is lifted above the dusty level of political and economic readjustments to its height and length and breadth as the experience of belonging to a "Beloved Community of Memory and Hope." In its own terms this is essentially a mystical interpretation of man's life as a member of the race, and is a profoundly moving and satisfying intimation of religion.[40]

This humanistic mysticism, however, does not remain for very long within the dimension of the human—it has also a cosmic dimension. The fascination produced in us by the emergence of the supreme religious leader is necessarily followed by a feeling of awe in the presence of the mysterious universe which has actually produced this prophet. The philosophic formulations of "integrating process" and "nisus of Space-Time" are then seen to be intellectually satisfying but religiously insufficient. They are completed only when the essential mystery of the universe is rendered "numinous" through the emergence of great souls incarnating universal qualities. The tremendous mystery of the universe which excites in us the mysticism of nature—that mystery is

---

[39] It is important to stress communion with universal values in mysticism, for all too often the mystical experience is presented as something utterly incommunicable and relevant only to the particular idiosyncrasy of the individual concerned. A philosophical correction of such a view may be obtained from Brand Blanshard: "Since identical laws govern our thinking and an identical end is at work in all of us, since the very existence of universals implies community in our objects, we have argued that the apparent severance between our minds does not in strictness hold, and that one identical mind is finding expression through them. 'The greater the spiritual activity within a man, the less is he able to ascribe this activity to himself.' If this is mysticism, then our doctrine is mystical."—*The Nature of Thought* (London, 1939), II, 180. The emergent evolutionist might perhaps wish to interpret "one identical mind" as "one identical creativity."

[40] Willard L. Sperry, *What We Mean by Religion*, p. 27.

pierced through the culmination in history of the religious giant who in his isolated heroic action communicates the light of his own spirit to the whole of humanity for all future time—in so far as men become aware of his significance. The mysticism of nature and the mysticism of personality are then merged into one mysticism—the dynamic mystery of the cosmos producing that person representing a universal quality so completely that we no longer know whether the person is lost in the quality or the quality lost in the person we venerate. The quality, the person, and the universe which sustains them may be "realized" in one intense flash of mystical experience.

This intimate union between the creativity of the universe and the religious giant may be expressed in terms of Bergson's evolutionary philosophy: "The mystic love of humanity . . . *is* this impetus itself communicated in its entirety to exceptional men who in their turn would fain impart it to all humanity." [41]

We commune, then, with an order of reality made up, to be sure, of those levels of organization studied by evolutionary philosophers, but this order is accessible to religion through the emergence in historical time of the supreme personality sustained by all these lower levels. Thus our religious attachment to a person is never free from a cosmic relation. Even Felix Adler, founder of the Ethical Culture movement, felt this to be the essence of religion:

> Religion in a broad sense may be taken to mean any cause in which we are supremely interested. But in its more special signification it

[41] Bergson, *op. cit.,* p. 223. Whether the creativity of the universe is ever wholly communicated to even the greatest saints is a question which may be raised. This is the way Paul Weiss puts it, though a study of his philosophy is beyond the scope of this work: "A mystic is to be known by his mastery of the field which he and God constitute and through which they act." *Modes of Being* (Southern Illinois University Press, 1958), p. 362. As previously noted, Bergson's mystical views are related more closely to those of the East than to those of the Christian West. See Huston Smith, *The Religions of Man* (New York, 1958): "As nature's agent, *Tao* bears a resemblance to Bergson's *élan vital;* as her orderer, it parallels to some extent the *lex aeterna* of the Classical West, the eternal law of nature in accord with which the universe operates." P. 177.

means a cosmic faith—not only the desire to improve conditions among men in this little human colony that dwells upon one of the smallest planets of the universe, but an outreaching toward the vast scheme of things—a cosmic sense, not only of mystery but of trust. An ethical religion means interpreting this immense Nature about us in terms of the highest that human nature can be or think of.[42]

In other words, our relation to nature, our sense of oneness with it in those moments of exaltation so well described by scientists such as Flammarion and by nature poets, does not reach its full emotional value until we perceive nature as the ground of that creativity which pervades it—of that dynamic creativity which culminates in man, yea, in the highest of the race. And likewise our relation to humanity, our mystical communion with its supreme exemplars, does not reach its full emotional value until we perceive these gigantesque figures as dominating points, as summit characters of nature. Emerson's ever-recurring metaphor of man acting "in accordance with Nature" is closely related to what we are trying to say. It means his intuition that the potentiality of nature reaches its highest fulfillment in the potency of the human mind. And this unified mysticism of nature and man in turn does not reach its fullest emotional value and fruition until we feel fascinated, overwhelmed, in fact, by the sense of inexhaustibility apparent in these supreme religious personalities— inexhaustibility present in the superabundant riches of the universe and in the glorious personalities it produces, inexhaustibility in the heights and depths of our spiritual communion with this universe moving in the direction of an ever greater manifestation of its energies and values in distinct, conscious incarnations.

Theodore Meyer Greene, referring to artistic greatness, stresses a similar note:

Greatness might, it seems to me now, be described helpfully in terms of the concept of inexhaustibility. One of the characteristics of truly great art in any medium is the fact that the most sensitive and informed critic can return to it again and again and always find in it formal relationships not previously observed, insights, perspectives and evaluations not previously noted or comprehended. A great

[42] Felix Adler, *Our Part in This World* (New York, 1946), pp. 65-66.

work of art is thus, as it were, a perpetual challenge to fresh discovery, a continuing stimulus to growth, an inexhaustible source of refreshment and delight.[43]

The life of a religious genius may be called a work of art inexhaustible in its essential character. The veneration and adoration of countless generations of men for saints, prophets, seers, and founders of religions is eloquent testimony to the inexhaustible quality incarnated in these supreme artists in the art of life. The mystery of the universe has become transformed in their sublime heights. The hidden depths of the cosmos have been illumined by the "numinous" quality of these great exemplars. The mysterious fascination of these supreme personalities—to use Rudolf Otto's terminology—is a never-ending source of insight, strength, courage, and ecstasy. Condemned for our imperfections, we are yet sustained by a superabundance of riches, by a revitalization which extends to us a mystical communion beyond the bounds of defeat, beyond the bounds of tragedy. There are still available to us moments of exaltation when the beauty and the glory of life glow with an ineffable fire in our souls.

And thus do we recognize the truth of William James's acute awareness of the meaning of religion:

> We shall see how infinitely passionate a thing religion at its highest flights can be. Like love, like wrath, like hope, ambition, jealousy, like every other instinctive eagerness and impulse, it adds to life an enchantment which is not rationally or logically deducible from anything else. . . . Religious feeling is thus an absolute addition to the subject's range of life. It gives him a new sphere of power. When the outward battle is lost, and the outer world disowns him, it redeems and vivifies an interior world which otherwise would be an empty vessel.[44]

[43] Theodore Meyer Greene, *The Arts and the Art of Criticism* (Princeton, 1947), p. xiii.
[44] William James, *The Varieties of Religious Experience,* pp. 47-48.

NOTE ON THE CONTRIBUTORS

EDWIN T. BUEHRER, former editor of *The Journal of Liberal Religion,* is minister, Third Unitarian Church, Chicago, Illinois.

JOHN HAYNES HOLMES is Minister Emeritus, The Community Church of New York, author of *Rethinking Religion* and many other works on religious liberalism.

J. HUTTON HYND is Buchanan Prizeman in Moral Philosophy, University of Glasgow, Scotland; Leader of the Ethical Culture Society of St. Louis, 1933-50; Instructor in Comparative Religion, Washington University, St. Louis, 1947-50; President, American Humanist Association, 1947-48; now affiliated with the Ethical Societies in Great Britain, and with Adult Education, H. M. Forces, University of Southampton, England.

JOHN A. IRVING is Professor and Chairman, Department of Philosophy, Victoria College, University of Toronto; author of *Science and Values* (1952); coauthor of *American Philosophy Today and Tomorrow* (1935); *The Teaching of Philosophy* (1950); *The Heritage of Western Culture* (1952); *Architects of Modern Thought* (1955); *The Culture of Contemporary Canada* (1957); editor and coauthor of *The Values of Life* (1948); *Philosophy in Canada* (1952); *The Light and the Flame* (1956); contributor to scientific, literary, and philosophical periodicals.

LESTER MONDALE is Leader, Philadelphia Ethical Society, author of *The Unitarian Way of Life, Three Unitarian Philosophies of Religion, Values in World Religions.*

N. A. NIKAM, M.A. (Cantab.), St. John's College, Cambridge, England, is Professor of Philosophy, Mysore University, India; Secretary, Indian Philosophical Congress; Member, UNESCO International Committee on (1) Enquiry into the Teaching of Philosophy, (2) International Committee for the Preparation of a Source Book of Documents of Human Rights; Fulbright and

Ford Foundation Scholar and Visiting Fellow, Yale University, 1952-53; Member, Executive Committee of the International Institute of Philosophy, Paris.

KENNETH L. PATTON is Minister, The Charles Street Universalist Meeting House, Boston, Massachusetts; author of *The Visitor and Hello Man, Beyond Doubt, Strange Seed, Man's Hidden Search, Man is the Meaning*.

NEWTON P. STALLKNECHT is Chairman, Department of Philosophy and Director, School of Letters at Indiana University. He is author of *Studies in the Philosophy of Creation with special reference to Bergson and Whitehead; Strange Seas of Thought, studies in William Wordsworth's philosophy of man and nature;* (with Robert S. Brumbaugh) *The Spirit of Western Philosophy,* and *The Compass of Philosophy*. He is a frequent contributor to philosophical journals and to journals in the fields of English literature and criticism.

ALFRED P. STIERNOTTE was Post-Doctoral Fellow in Philosophy, Yale University, 1952-54; author of *God and Space-Time, Deity in the Philosophy of Samuel Alexander,* and *Frederick May Eliot: An Anthology;* Assistant Professor of Philosophy, Quinnipiac College, Hamden, Connecticut.

HENRY NELSON WIEMAN, Professor Emeritus, The University of Chicago, is visiting distinguished professor, Southern Illinois University, Carbondale, Illinois; author of *American Philosophies of Religion, Man's Ultimate Commitment,* and many other works on religion.

BIBLIOGRAPHY

Adler, Felix. *Our Part in this World*. New York, 1946.

Alexander, Samuel. *Philosophical and Literary Pieces*. London, 1939.

————. *Space, Time, and Deity*. New York, 1950.

Atkinson, B. (ed.). *The Complete Essays and Writings of Ralph Waldo Emerson*. New York, 1940.

Aurobindo, Śri. *The Life Divine*. Calcutta, 1949, 1951.

————. *The Mother*. Pondicherry, 1949.

————. *The Synthesis of Yoga*. Madras, 1948.

Bahadur, His Highness Śri Jaya Chamarajendra Wadiyar. *Dattatreya: The Way and the Goal*. London, 1957.

Bennett, C. A. *A Philosophical Study of Mysticism*. New Haven, 1923.

Bergson, Henri. *The Two Sources of Morality and Religion*. New York, 1935.

Blanshard, B. *The Nature of Thought*. London, 1939.

Blood, B. P. *Pluriverse, an Essay in the Philosophy of Pluralism*. Boston, 1920.

Bradley, F. H. *Appearance and Reality*. Oxford, 1930.

Brightman, E. S. *Person and Reality*. New York, 1958.

Buber, M. *Eclipse of God*. New York, 1952.

————. *I and Thou*. Edinburgh, 1937.

Burtt, E. A. *Man Seeks the Divine*. New York, 1957.

Camus, Albert. *The Rebel*. New York, 1954.

Chaix-Ruy, J. *Les Dimensions de L'Etre et du Temps*. Paris, 1953.

Cook, Joseph. "The Physical Tangibleness of the Moral Law," *Boston Monday Lectures*. Boston, 1879.

Cooke, G. W. *Ralph Waldo Emerson*. Boston, 1881.

Coulson, C. A. "Mathematics and Beauty," *The Listener*, 43 (1950), 784-85.

Davies, A. P. *The Faith of an Unrepentant Liberal*. Boston, 1946.

Demos, Raphael (ed.). *The Dialogues of Plato*. New York, 1937.

Edman, Irwin. *Four Ways of Philosophy*. New York, 1937.

Einstein, A. *The World as I see it.* New York, 1949.

Emerson, R. W. *Conduct of Life.* Boston, 1886.

————. *Essays, First Series.* Boston, 1888.

————. *Lecture on the Times.* Boston, 1898.

————. *Lectures and Biographical Sketches.* Boston, 1884.

————. *Nature, Addresses, and Lectures.* Boston, 1884.

————. *Society and Solitude.* Boston, 1886.

Flammarion, Camille. *Astronomie Populaire.* Paris, 1922.

————. *Popular Astronomy.* New York, 1907.

Forsyth, T. M. *God and the World.* London, 1952.

Gandhi, M. K. *Hindu Dharma.* Ahmedabad, 1950.

George, F. H. and Handlon, J. H. "A Language for Perceptual Analysis," *Psychological Review,* 64 (1957), 14-25.

Greene, T. M. *Our Cultural Heritage.* Houston, 1956.

————. *The Arts and the Art of Criticism.* Princeton, 1947.

Hastings, J. (ed.). *Encyclopedia of Religion and Ethics,* Vol. 9. New York, 1917.

Hocking, W. E. *The Meaning of God in Human Experience.* New Haven, 1912.

Holmes, J. H. "A Modern Faith," *The Beacon Song and Service Book.* Boston, 1935, p. 72.

————. *Rethinking Religion.* New York, 1938.

Hudson, J. W. "The Religion of Emerson," *The Sewanee Review,* 28 (1920), 203-12.

Hügel, F. von. *The Mystical Element of Religion.* New York, 1927.

Hughes, T. H. *The Philosophical Basis of Mysticism.* Edinburgh, 1937.

Hume, R. E. (ed.). *The Thirteen Principal Upanishads.* London, 1931.

Hutcheon, R. J. *Frankness in Religion.* New York, 1929.

Inge, W. R. *Mysticism in Religion.* Chicago, 1948.

————. *God and the Astronomers.* New York, 1933.

Irving, J. A. *Science and Values.* Toronto, 1952.

James, William. *The Varieties of Religious Experience.* New York, 1902.

Jaspers, K. *The Origin and Goal of History.* New Haven, 1953.

————. *The Way to Wisdom.* New Haven, 1954.

Johnson, W. E. *Logic.* Cambridge, 1921.

Jones, R. M. *Studies in Mystical Religion*. London, 1923.

————. *New Studies in Mystical Religion*. New York, 1927.

Jung, C. G. *Answer to Job*. London, 1954.

Kahler, Erich. *The Tower and the Abyss*. New York, 1957.

Kaufmann, W. *Existentialism from Dostoevsky to Sartre*. New York, 1957.

Kraft, V. *The Vienna Circle*. New York, 1953.

Laird, John. *Theism and Cosmogony*. London, 1940.

————. "Theism and Hypertheism," *Harvard Theological Review*, 36 (1943), 63-81.

Lamont, C. *The Philosophy of Humanism*. New York, 1958.

Leuba, J. H. *God or Man?* London, 1934.

————. *The Psychology of Religious Mysticism*. New York, 1925.

Lyman, E. W. *The Meaning and Truth of Religion*. New York, 1933.

Macintosh, D. C. *The Problem of Religious Knowledge*. New York, 1940.

McKellar, Peter. *Imagination and Thinking*. London, 1957.

Macmurray, J. *Idealism against Religion*. London, 1944.

Mallik, Gurdial. *Divine Dwellers in the Desert*. Bombay, 1949.

Marcel, Gabriel. *Being and Having*. London, 1949.

————. *Man Against Mass Society*. Chicago, 1952.

————. *The Philosophy of Existence*. London, 1948.

Marquette, J. de. *Introduction to Comparative Mysticism*. New York, 1949.

Millay, E. St. *Renascence and Other Poems*. New York, 1940.

Moore, C. A. (ed.). *Essays in East-West Philosophy*. Honolulu, 1951.

Muirhead, J. H. and S. Radhakrishnan (eds.). *Contemporary Indian Philosophy*. London, 1952.

Northrop, F. S. C. *The Meeting of East and West*. New York, 1946.

Norton, C. E. (ed.). *The Correspondence of Thomas Carlyle and Ralph Waldo Emerson*. Boston, 1883.

Otto, R. *Mysticism East and West*. New York, 1932.

————. *The Idea of the Holy*. London, 1952.

Parker, T. *The American Scholar*. Boston, 1907.

Passmore, John. *A Hundred Years of Philosophy*. New York, 1957.

Patton, K. L. *Man is the Meaning*. Boston, 1956.

Paul, S. *Emerson's Angle of Vision*. Cambridge, 1952.

Potter, C. F. *Creative Personality*. New York, 1950.

Pratt, J. B. *India and Its Faith*. Boston, 1915.

——. *The Religious Consciousness*. New York, 1946.

Radhakrishnan, S. *Eastern Religions and Western Thought*. London, 1940.

——. *Recovery of Faith*. New York, 1955.

—— (ed.). *The Principal Upaniṣads*. New York, 1953.

Ramanāśraman, Śri. *Maharshi's Gospel*. Tiruvannamalai, India, 1949.

Raven, C. E. *Natural Religion and Christian Theology*. Cambridge, 1953.

——. *Experience and Interpretation*. Cambridge, 1953.

Sartre, Jean-Paul. *Being and Nothingness*. New York, 1956.

——. *Existentialism*. New York, 1947.

——. *Nausea*. Norfolk, Conn., 1949.

Schlick, Moritz. *Philosophy of Nature*. New York, 1949.

Schweitzer, Albert. *Indian Thought and its Development*. London, 1936.

——. *Out of My Life and Thought*. New York, 1949.

Sinnott, E. W. *Matter, Mind and Man*. New York, 1957.

——. *The Biology of the Spirit*. New York, 1955.

Smith, H. *The Religions of Man*. New York, 1958.

Smith, M. *An Introduction to the History of Mysticism*. New York, 1930.

Smuts, J. C. *Holism and Evolution*. New York, 1926.

Sneath, E. H. *At One with the Invisible*. New York, 1921.

Some New Letters of Śri Aurobindo. Pondicherry, 1949.

Sperry, W. L. *What We Mean by Religion*. New York, 1940.

Stace, W. T. *Religion and the Modern Mind*. Philadelphia and New York, 1952.

——. *Time and Eternity*. Princeton, 1952.

Stallknecht, N. P. "Being in Becoming: A Theory of Human Freedom," *The Review of Metaphysics*, 8 (1955), 633-41.

——. "Beyond the Concrete," *The Review of Metaphysics*, 7 (1954), 144-55.

——. "Gabriel Marcel and the Human Situation," *The Review of Metaphysics*, 7 (1954), 661-67.

—— and R. S. Brumbaugh. *The Compass of Philosophy*. New York, 1954.

Stern, Alfred. *Sartre: His Philosophy and Psychoanalysis*. New York, 1953.

Stiernotte, A. P. *God and Space-Time*. New York, 1954.

Sullivan, H. S. *The Interpersonal Theory of Psychiatry*. New York, 1953.

Suzuki, D. T. *An Introduction to Zen Buddhism*. London, 1948.

————. *Essays in Zen Buddhism*. London, 1950.

————. *Mysticism: Christian and Buddhist*. New York, 1957.

————. "Zen: A Reply to Hu Shih," *Philosophy East and West*, 3 (1953), 25-46.

Tillich, P. *Systematic Theology*, Vol. I. Chicago, 1951.

————. *The Shaking of the Foundations*. New York, 1948.

Underhill, E. *Mysticism*. London, 1930.

Urmson, J. O. *Philosophical Analysis*. Oxford, 1956.

Venkataraman, T. N. *Talks with Ramana Maharshi*. Tiruvannamalai, India, 1955.

Vogt, von O. *The Primacy of Worship*. Boston, 1958.

Wach, J. *Types of Religious Experience, Christian and Non-Christian*. Chicago, 1951.

Wahl, Jean. *Traité de Métaphysique*. Paris, 1953.

————. *Philosopher's Way*. New York, 1948.

Watts, A. W. *The Supreme Identity*. New York, 1950.

Weiss, P. *Man's Freedom*. New Haven, 1950.

————. *Modes of Being*. Carbondale, 1958.

Whitehead, A. N. *Process and Reality*. New York, 1929.

————. *Religion in the Making*. New York, 1926.

————. *Science and the Modern World*. New York, 1929.

Whitman, Walt. *Leaves of Grass*. Philadelphia, 1900.

Whyte, L. L. *Accent on Form*. New York, 1954.

Wieman, H. N. *Man's Ultimate Commitment*. Carbondale, 1958.

————. *Methods of Private Religious Living*. New York, 1928.

————. *Religious Experience and Scientific Method*. New York, 1926.

————. *The Source of Human Good*. Chicago, 1945.

Williams, D. D. *What Present-Day Theologians are Thinking*. New York, 1952.

Wittgenstein, L. *Tractatus Logico-Philosophicus*. New York, 1951.

INDEX